Have fun on the course!

Job Remiles

The Rules of Golf 2004-2005 is used with the permission of the
United States Golf Association. To order the complete version of
The Rules of Golf 2004-2005 or the Golf Rules in Brief,
contact the USGA Order Department at (800) 336-4446.

Library of Congress Cataloging-in-Publication Data is available

Renslow, John A.
IN THE LOOP: A Crash Course in the Golf Culture
by John Renslow

ISBN 0-9747945-1-1

IN THE LOOP

A Crash Course
in the Golf Culture

John Renslow

PGA Golf Professional

WOLSNER PUBLISHING COMPANY
Brentwood, California

To Leigh, Lauren, Laynee and the Player to be named Later.

Thank you for supporting my habit.

Table of Contents

Introduction

Whether in Sport or in Industry, cultures are created by their participants. A type of behavior and manner of speech evolve into something that only those within the culture can easily decipher. The words are common throughout the English-speaking world; however, within a culture these phrases take on a whole new meaning. The mannerisms are more specifically suited to the activity and this behavior is accepted and encouraged.

The world of Golf has just such a Culture. Other sports have unique environments, but there doesn't seem to be the same barriers to the information. These barriers are not structured. There are no borders. The simple fact is that when one begins to play the game there is no way to gather enough information in the time allowed to avoid feeling like a foreigner. The information can be elusive and perhaps too exhaustive to have someone sit down and talk you through it.

As you contemplate playing the game many of these ideas and idiosyncrasies won't even come to mind. Your initial area of concern is ability and skill level. The idea that if one is able to play a credible game of golf then the respect from fellow golfers is sure to follow. The notions of behavior, what you should say, where one should stand, or how you drive a golf cart is not part of the thinking process.

You will soon discover that the skill level or athletic ability of a player comes in a distant second place to how you behave and speak (or don't speak) on the course. There are many members of Country Clubs and weekend golf warriors who are miserable players. Veterans whose golf swings resemble violent acts rather than rhythmical motions, but they are 'in the loop'. They know how to behave in the culture.

They know for example, that playing quickly is more important than playing well. A good player may have a difficult time being accepted into a group if they play slow. Where as a player with below average ability is grafted into a group quickly if they are able to play at a good pace and know how to have a good time.

Since my teens I have been playing this wonderful game. Fortunately, my first job was at a golf course in Northern California where the Head Golf Professional was a PGA & Senior PGA Tour player. His son, Rob Boldt, (who also became a PGA Tour player) took me under his wing and brought me into the fold. Now I am a PGA Member and golf Club Professional. It has been my pleasure to teach the culture, the mechanics, and the history of the game to hundreds of Students and Employees over the last fifteen years.

This book is a digest of experience, definitions, and stories that will help you to fit in with friends who play the game, as well as those that you will meet on the Course. Because when it comes to down to it, it doesn't matter how you play, it's how you look.

Chapter 1

A DAY ON THE LINKS

"I lost my #8 iron", said the voice over the phone.

It is common for players to leave a golf club behind during a round of golf. Perhaps the ball was a good distance from the golf cart and the golfer was unsure of the correct club choice. A player might bring an assortment of clubs and then choose the best one when it is time to hit. After the golfer has played the shot, the clubs are gathered and returned to the golf bag. Occasionally, during this transition, a golf club is abandoned. These clubs are often found by a player from another group and left in the care of the Golf Shop Staff.

"What type of golf club is it?" I asked. "Is it graphite or steel? What brand is it?"

"I don't know, let me go check", was the reply.

Off to the garage he went. Pause. Pause. Bang. Crash. Ouch. Pause. Pause.

"Oh, I got it! I got it!" he exclaimed. "It's a patent pending."

Over the years I have found that one of the best ways to serve customers, is to provide them with information. We all tend to get a little skittish about the unknown. Where is this? Where do I go after that?

It is difficult to play host to your guests or look comfortable in your group unless you know a little bit of what is going to happen. This chapter will give you an overview of what to expect on a normal day at the average golf course. What you have on your side is that no two courses are alike. To have a few questions is normal. You won't be expected to know everything. Also in your favor is that in all likelihood, if you have guests, they don't know any more about a certain golf course than you do.

Arrival Time -

Plan to arrive at the Golf Course with enough time to check-in (register) with the Golf Shop/Starter at least 30 minutes prior to your Starting Time. This half an hour will be composed of three parts. First, you will need ten minutes to get unloaded (people and golf bags out of the car) and processed through the Golf Shop. Then it will take the next ten minutes to warm up (hit several range balls and a few putts). Finally, you will need to arrive at the First Tee ten minutes prior to your Starting Time to check-in with the Starter. The 'starting time' is truly measured by the moment the ball is in the air. So, you can't arrive on the First Tee exactly at the appointed time. By the time all of the players in your group get to the tee, go through all of the necessary pre-swing machinations and hit, the next golfers will arrive with you still standing there. Their hope is that you won't do this all day.

For those of you who need more time to warm up, or feel like getting breakfast or lunch that's fine. Get there earlier and head into the Golf Shop. Let the Staff know your plans and ask them when you should check in and pay your fees. This will really impress the Shop Staff, because they will think you know what you're doing.

In the event of an unforeseen delay that would cause you to arrive less than thirty minutes prior to you Starting Time, there is a certain amount of tolerance. Each course is different, but you will probably be safe if there is at least a fifteen-minute window. However, you have just missed any opportunity to hit range balls, practice your putting, look around the golf shop, or grab a beverage before you head out. You just want to get in the shop, apologize, pay your fees and get to the First Tee as soon as possible. If your group is two or larger, the smart thing to do is divide and conquer. For example, with two players, one of you should take care of the unloading and loading of golf bags and the other should go pay greens fees for the two of you in the Golf Shop. This may or may not be convenient for you, but that is not in the forefront under these conditions. The Golf Shop Staff is like an Air Traffic Control tower and they are trying to keep you in the pattern.

Heaven forbid that you and/or your group arrive within a few minutes of your Starting Time. As soon as it is possible, call and notify the Golf Shop Staff. Once in the Golf Shop you must simply throw yourself on the mercy of the court, because here is the deal. Again, think of the Starter or Golf Shop like Air Traffic Control. Planes are scheduled to arrive and depart on time. How many of you have gone to the Airport on time, checked-in on time and were prepared for boarding, only to gaze with anticipation toward a jet way with no plane? The flight has been delayed. Anticipation turns to annoying. Annoying turns into anger. You with me? This is exactly what would happen if the Starter holds up play for you. Lets use a railroad scenario. How many of us, if late to the Station, would expect the engineer, crew and passengers to wait for us to arrive? The train is leaving the Station. This doesn't mean that you don't get to play golf. It just means that you wait for the next train.

Bag Drop -

As you drive onto the Property, there should be signage for what is called a Bag Drop. This is the spot at which you should stop your car and unload your golf bag. We need to pause here for a moment and discuss security. Use common sense. If the Bag Drop is unattended and/or this is not a secure place to leave your Golf Bag, then by all means continue driving to the Parking Lot and keep your Bag with you.

At the better Course, the Bag Drop is the way to go. Once the bag is removed from your car, the Golf Service Staff will get the Bag down to the Golf Shop area or on a Golf Cart if you prefer. Feel free to ask questions. The Service Staff knows where everything is and you won't look like a rookie if you ask; "Where is the Pro Shop?" "Do you have a Locker Room?" "Where is the Driving Range?" If appropriate, pop the Service Staff a few bucks. Allow the rest of your party to head for the Club House, close the trunk, and you're off to park the car.

Where to Park -

Ideally, take a moment to figure out where you will be at the end of the day. This could be the final hole or the Golf Shop or the Bar. Park as close to that spot as possible. There is one big thing, however, to consider before make a decision. Ask yourself, am I about to park my car in a location that could be ground zero for falling golf balls?

Two words on PC -

This might seem trivial, but it is one of the small things that will set you apart from the rookies, not to mention impress other players. When playing a Private Club, use the Locker Room to change your shoes. It is an unwritten Club taboo to change your shoes in the parking lot. This would be looked on as a Public Course or 'Muni' maneuver and you could be viewed as a commoner. One more thing on Private Clubs. Many Private Clubs do not take cash. This is how the Club maintains its exemptions from many State regulations. Each Member has an account to which purchases are billed and then paid on a monthly basis. So, when possible, ask your host what the Club's policy is regarding purchases. When a facility is "cash only", offer to pay your host directly for a purchase on his/her account. If your host does the classy thing, they will 'take care' (pay for) your incidentals. If not, just figure in some tax and pay the cheapskate.

Inside the Shop -

Before you arrive at the Counter in the Golf Shop you need to decide a few things; are you low on golf balls?, do you need a new glove?, are you going to hit some range balls?, and the high ticket item, are you going to walk or ride? An interesting quirk of human behavior is the inability to prepare for something that requires little or no preparation. For me it's the Grocery Store. After being on the planet for a few decades and having been in the Grocery Store more times than necessary for the average waistline, I still return a dumfounded look when asked whether I would like 'paper or plastic.' When the Staff poses the question "Are you going to walk or ride?", you should be ready to respond. Better yet, tell them before you are asked. That type of preparation will not go unnoticed.

Greens Fee rates vary greatly. Prices will be all over the board depending upon the type of facility and the demographical area. A small Par 3 course may have a rate of just $6 for nine holes. This will graduate all the way up to the most famous Golf Courses charging over $300 for a round of golf. With many public golf courses, several rate categories have been established for golfers. Even though there are many different possibilities, the usual suspects are; a Standard Rate, a Junior Rate, a Senior Rate and a Twilight Rate. One set of these rates will relate to Weekends and another will be applied on Weekdays. The rates are distributed through promotional material or posted in the Golf Shop and often can be viewed via the Internet.

As with the average greens fee, the cost of a cart will vary from location to location with the average rate around $25. Golf Carts will accommodate two riders, but if you do not have a partner to share the fee, the Course will still rent the Cart. It's just that the rate may be the same either way. Each Golf Course will have its own policy on a reduced fee for a single rider. There are two schools of thought. One course will allow the 'single' rider to pay a reduced fee, even half of the total rate. The other will have a simple cart fee whether there are two riders or just one rider.

Unfair you say. Why should one rider have to pay the same rate as if two were riding in the cart? The Golf Course operator has a few valid arguments. 1) The cost to the Golf Course is the same regardless of the number of riders. 2) Reducing the rate translates to a loss of revenue for many courses who have a limited number of Golf Carts in the fleet. For instance, ABC Golf Course has 50 Golf Carts in the fleet. If all 50 were rented at half price for single riders, not only does the operator have half of normal revenue, but also others who want to ride cannot, because no more golf carts are available. And unfortunately, 3) there are some less than clever individuals who will inform the Golf Shop that only three of their four players would like to ride. There may be one genuine scenario like that in ten, but more than likely, on the second tee, all four butts are in the seats. Rather than hire Private Investigators, the single fee cart policy eliminates the issue. Therefore, if you play as a single or are the third of three players, just ask if they have a cart rate for single riders. *(See Chapter 6 for some important information on driving your golf cart).*

In summary, there is one main greens fee that needs to be paid. After that you have options; Cart? Merchandise? Range Balls? Inform the Golf Shop Attendant of your choices, hand over your credit card and you are on your way!

On the Driving Range -

This may seem sophomoric, but the first thing to figure out is the location of the Range Ball Dispenser. For properties that 'rent' range balls, the typical procedure is to purchase a token that is used in a large dispenser that looks like a big green soda machine. Once you have found the machine, find a container for the range balls -- usually a plastic pail. Place the container in position to receive balls from the machine before you take the token from your pockct. I wish I had a dollar for every time I've seen several dozen range balls erupting from the machine due to operator error. If the token is inserted before the buckct is in position, it looks like the California Lottery with all of those balls hopping around. Of course, in this event, you can just tell everyone that this was some type of mechanical glitch or a technical malfunction.

If you have driven a golf cart to the Driving Range pick a spot to park that will make it easy for you to go to your next location (probably the 1st Tee). Also, a Driving Range is a big place and you could have a healthy walk in front of you. The practice tee being used on a given day might be a hundred yards from where you parked your cart. Just take a selection of Clubs from your bag rather than lug the whole thing around. This is a veteran move.

The First Tee -

There are two ways that the First Tee is regulated. The first is by the use of a Public Address system and the second is through a Starter. A Starter is an individual who will stand on or near the Tee and inform each group when it is their time to begin.

Get to the First Tee five to ten minutes before your starting time. If there is a delay the Golf Shop should inform you when you check in.

When the Group in front of you is out of range, or the Starter gives you the official 'okey-dokey', then go ahead and hit your ball.

Mulligans: Although you won't find this anywhere in the Rules of Golf Book, there is an unwritten rule: the First Tee 'do over', or Mulligan. Frankly, this is more the move of a commoner. Part of being a Veteran in the game is accepting the fact that you are the only one responsible for hitting your golf shot. Therefore, you find it and hit it again. The one possible exception; there is no opportunity to warm-up. If the Course has no driving range or time does not allow and it won't hold up your group or the group behind you, take a quick survey of the other players ('do you mind?') and proceed with caution.

On the Course -

The most important thing that you can do on the Golf Course is to play quickly. Remember, what you will learn from this book is how to have the confidence of a veteran. You will appear to know what you're doing. Trust me. Ironically, a player is more vilified for being a slow-player than for not playing well.

After playing baseball in Junior College, I had the opportunity to spend some time with some of the coaches and players in a professional baseball organization. When they talked about recruiting baseball players the number one thing on their list was speed. The rationale is that hitting has slumps, pitching has good days and bad days, but speed comes to the ballpark everyday.

If you play poorly, your group will not know if you are a bad golfer or if you're just having a bad day. In fact, you will undoubtedly receive some words of encouragement to spur you on. This will not be a detriment when it comes time to invite you out for another round of golf. However, even if you are a skilled player, slow-play will make it tough to find a partner. Slow-play comes to the ballpark everyday and your reputation will precede you. Once again, how you behave, how you interact, how you treat others, is more important than how you play.

At the Turn --

Customarily the golf course will have an opportunity at the mid-way point of the round to take a moment and gather any required nourishment. Healthy meals like hot dogs and burgers will be available, along with a cold-cut sandwich or an energy bar.

A couple of veteran points to address. First of all, speed is of the essence. In fact, many properties will have a radio or telephone installed on the course so that you can place an order before you arrive at the turn. Go ahead and use it. Like a good Server, ask the players in your group if they would like anything at the 'Snack Shack' or 'Snack Bar'. Then pick up the phone and place the order.

At the Snack Bar, those that placed an order get their refreshment. Anyone who needs a 'comfort break' may do so and then it's off to the back-nine.

There is something else that you need to know if you are playing with experienced players. Specifically if you are in a group with some private club veterans, I want you to be aware of something. Most golf veterans enjoy a good bet. We don't like a bad bet, that would be gambling. This includes the determination of who will buy the snacks at the Turn. A game of dice will decide which player in the group will pay the entire bill. The name of the game is 'Liar's Dice'.

Here is how it works. Each player has a cup that contains 5 dice. Shake the cup and place it with the mouth of the cup down. Don't lift the cup. Now, gently tilt the cup so that you are the only person who can see the dice. The object is to 'out guess' or identify the exact number of a particular digit that is face up on all of the dice.

This includes your cup and all of your opponent's cups. The digit 6, of course, has the highest value and the digit 1 is 'wild' and can be used as any other digit.

One player makes a bid, guessing how many of a given number have been rolled. If I were starting, I could bid "four 5s", betting that the total of natural 5s plus any 'wild' 1's would be equal to or greater than four. Once I make my bid, the next player has two options, he/she can "raise the bid" or he/she can challenge me by calling my bluff. To raise the bid the next 'call' must be either a larger quantity of any number ("five 3's") or the same quantity of a higher valued digit ("four 6's"). Calls are made in order. The order can be set however you prefer, but after it has been set, it does not change.

When a player decides that the previous call is highly improbable (or a lie), the bluff is called and all the dice are revealed. Starting with the one to call the bluff, everyone reveals his or her dice. If the bid is equaled or exceeded, the Challenger loses one of their dice. When the bid is shy or short of the called number, the 'Liar' loses one of their dice. At this point a new round begins, the players roll their dice, and secretly take look at their own dice.

At the turn this continues until one player is out of dice. There is no need to continue. They pay for the snacks. Naturally, the full version of this game is popular for the 19th hole (upon completing the round). More rounds are necessary, as each 'Liar' will lose all of his or her dice. Play then continues until only one player has dice.

After Your Round --

Take a brief moment and shake hands with the individuals in your group. It's a Golf thing. Remove your hat, extend your arm and give their hand a good firm squeeze. While you're at it ask them what they would like to do next. Essentially, you have two options: slamming the trunk and getting out of Dodge, or hanging out at the Course and talk about the round whilst enjoying the beverage of your choice. Usually, players opt for the latter. This is known as the 19th hole.

The next step may seem obvious, but you would not believe how many people struggle with this. When you have completed your Round...Get off of the Golf Course. People sometimes have a conversation, count the number of strokes they made on that hole, sit in the cart and tally up their score, yada, yada, yada. Meanwhile, the Group behind is leaning on a club watching a show with little entertainment value. Get out of the way. Once you have left the eighteenth green, you can do whatever you want -- clean your golfbag, or get the calculator out. Granted this is one of those things in life that you will never be thanked for. It's just the right thing to do.

Inside the Clubhouse, you will be able to Post your Score (see Chapter 12). As well as hit the Restroom/Locker Room and wash-up. Then it's onward to the Grill. You and your Group may order some Potato Skins, or the like, and a frosty beverage and engage in stimulating conversation for a while. It is then time to head home.

A brief inventory is a good idea. Got my clubs? Got my hat? Got my cell phone? Got my wallet? Okay, cool, oops what about my keys.....

Chapter 2

THE WAITING LIST

One fateful day at the Lincoln Park Golf Course in San Francisco, a rather rotund man, without a reservation, wanted to play a round of golf. He came into the Golf Shop and placed his name among many others on the Waiting List. As is often the case at a public golf course, on a weekend, in California, one can wait for hours. After standing by for quite some time, the man complained that he did not feel well. Shortly after, this unlucky fellow collapsed between the double doors of the entryway to the Golf Shop. He remained down for quite some time and before medical attention arrived, another patron leaned through the doorway, looked over and past him to shout, "Was he ahead of me on the Waiting List?"

If you have not yet made reservations for dinner, you may arrive at a restaurant and wait for a table to become available. The Server takes your name and writes it down on a list. When the appropriate table is vacant your name is called and you are led to your seat.

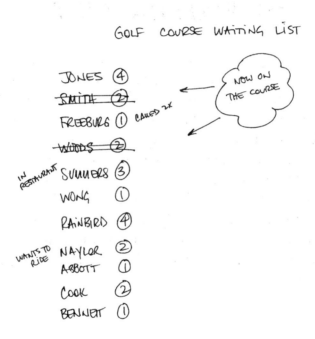

Each Golf Course that is available to the public will create a Waiting or Stand-by list on a daily basis. If you want to play golf, but do not have a reservation, you need to get on this list. Again, in concept, the Golf Course Waiting List is like that of a restaurant and you are waiting for an 'open table'.

Let me explain the mechanics of this. The Golf Course has Starting Times or Reservations that are taken prior to the day of play. On that day, if you have not made a reservation in advance, you are waiting for someone who has a Reserved Starting Time to leave a vacancy by not showing up. Or, for a reservation of a certain size to reduce its number of players. For example, the Smith party has reserved a Starting Time for Four Players at 8:20 a.m.. On that day, Uncle Dave is having back problems. So, when they get to the Golf Course for their Starting Time, they arrive with only three players. When the Golf Shop Staff is notified of this, they refer to that day's Waiting List and identify the first player to register alone (called a 'Single'). Next, the player is paged to report to the Golf Shop. This 'single' then pays a Greens Fee, and is 'paired up' with the other three players.

The procedure works the same way with two, three or four players, but this differs with the restaurant analogy in that the Golf Shop Staff is trying to fill a Starting Time that can accommodate exactly four people. So, if there is availability for one player, the Staff will identify the first 'Single', who will then receive preference regardless of his or her placement on the list.

When this is going to occur no one knows. Obviously, it is not reasonable to ask the Golf Shop Staff 'what the odds are' of getting on the golf course, or worse, specifically when they think its going to take place. This question has come up before the day has even arrived. That is like asking one of the Golf Shop Staff when Uncle Dave's back is going to hurt. Somewhere, somehow I suppose it is possible to calculate the odds or chances of this happening, but even that would change on a daily basis.

For the sake of illustration, lets say that it is Saturday morning. The Starter's Tee-Sheet is booked until 4:15 p.m.. Two players walk in to the shop at 10:00 a.m., without a reservation and would like to play. If every group or player that has a reservation were to arrive, these two could play after 4:15p.m. "But", you say, "Couldn't they just 'squeeze' us out between some of the groups that have a reservation?" Well, most likely, no. Two reasons; one, this would push back someone who already has a reservation (its not their fault) and two, to be fair, this procedure would then need to be applied to everyone on the Waiting List. Where would we be then?

That having been said there are some things that you should know to give yourself the best opportunity to get on the Golf Course. First off, it is better to wait with a smaller number of people. Remember, you are waiting for someone that has a Reservation to be absent. So, if you are a party of four players (with four being the typical capacity for one Starting Time) an entire Starting Time reservation has to open up. On a weekend, in the Golf Business, that is not going to happen very often.

People rarely cancel weekend times. If reservations were made a month ahead of time and then the players can't make it, they will call their Uncle Ralph and give the Reservation to him. Failure to appear without notice is even more unusual for a weekend time. It is common though, for a four-player reservation to arrive at the golf course with only three players or even two.

As a single person you have a good opportunity to find an opening or with two players you have a reasonable shot. However, with more people than that (sets of 3 or 4 waiting), you are just rolling the dice.

In the past a Golf Course would hold or set aside a 'Starter' or 'Walk-on' Starting Time. This allowed space for the Starter to get a person on the golf course who 'walked-on' without a reservation, or if the Starter got behind on the schedule, it gave them some room to get back on time. But the CPA can't account for an open reservation. With the growing number of Golf Courses and the competition for players, today's Operators can't afford to leave open times even though they might fill.

Here's what you should do. When your schedule allows for a round of golf, but you know that a reservation is not available, you can still go to the course and get on the Waiting List. Prior to doing this, phone your specific course and ask a couple of questions. First, what is their procedure or policy for a Waiting List? Usually, this is a first come, first served basis. A Golf Course is typically not going to put someone on the Waiting List prior to the day of play. If you were able to put yourself on a Waiting List and know when you were going to play, that would be a Reservation.

Secondly, ask the Golf Shop Staff if there is a Tournament or Group Event on the day that you would like to play. When a Tournament or Group Event makes a reservation, they guarantee a certain number of players and often pay in advance. You will not be able to find an available starting time when a large group has guaranteed reservations.

On the day that you want to play, mosey into the Golf Shop and inform the Staff that you do not have a reservation. Tell them the number of players that you have and give them your name. As stated previously, if at all possible, try not to ask them how long the wait will be. They can make a guess based on experience, but they don't really know.

Here is some insight into avoiding a frustrating scenario. The Golf Shop Staff is between a rock and a hard place trying to make a call on this one. If they tell you two hours, you won't like that. That's a long time to wait and you'll want to discuss the future with someone who knows little more about the future than you do. So, the Staff doesn't often choose to say that. Also, if the Staff member says thirty minutes and it ends up being an hour you'll be upset, because they told you half an hour. So, the Staff doesn't feel comfortable stating this either. This might be alright if it were only one customer, but the average public Golf Shop will see 250 - 275 people every day.

Its a funny thing about human nature, we feel uncomfortable with open ended stuff. Any piece of information will put us more at ease.

Try this. Just ask the Golf Shop Staff if it's busy. This way you are not putting the Staff on the spot by asking them to predict the future. You are asking them to tell you the present. In fact, because the question is so much more realistic, you will probably get more information than you bargained for.

Go hit some range balls. Roll a few putts. Depending on the time of day have some breakfast or lunch. Relax. Do not pace in the Golf Shop. Try to stay out of the Golf Shop (unless you're shopping), but within earshot of the Public Address system. The Staff will not forget about you. They want to get you on the Golf Course, too.

Chapter 3

FACILITY TYPES

There is a very exclusive Club in the South that hosts a Major Championship. One of the benefits for the winner is a Membership in the Club. Rumor has it that one day, Mr. Champion, a former winner, made his way to the Club to play a round of golf with his eldest son. Mr. Champion's son is a very good player in his own right, with victories in significant amateur events. The story goes that when Mr. Champion arrived at the gate, he informed the Guard that he and his son were there to play golf. At this news, the Guard responded, "Mr. Champion, as a Member you are welcome to play, however, we cannot welcome your guest".

Golf Course Properties come in many different shapes and sizes. This not only includes the design and topography, but also the manner in which they are managed. One Golf Course may be open to the public; another may be available to anyone on a daily basis and also sell 'memberships' on an 'annual basis.' Others may be for the use of its Membership only. First, I will discuss the types of properties from a 'playing' standpoint, and then, I will touch on the intricate world of Golf Course Management.

GOLF COURSE TYPES:

Size matters. This holds true when it comes to establishing Par and identifying Golf Courses. With most golf courses in the United States calculated in yards, there are some general guidelines using these measurements. Generally speaking, for men, a hole that is fewer than 250 yards is designated as a Par 3. Traditionally, this means that the advanced player will make one swing to get the ball on the putting green and then hit two putts to get the ball in the hole. This is also known as 'hitting a green in regulation.' Holes with a distance of more than 250 yards, but fewer than 450 yards, are designated as a Par 4 and if the distance is greater than 450 yards, it is known as a Par 5. These are not absolute, but you won't see too many situations outside these guidelines. Now on occasion, a Committee might decide to give a Par 6 moniker to the hole which has a length over 600 yards. However, even if the hole is this long, most courses stay with the traditional Par 5.

For most properties, the total for Par is 72. Typically, the course is composed of 18 holes; this breaks down to ten par 4 holes, four par 3 holes, and four par 5 holes. This is a type of Regulation Golf Course. A *Regulation Golf Course* is any 9-hole or 18-hole golf course that includes a variety of par 3, par 4 and par 5 holes that stay within these distance parameters; a 9-hole facility must be at least 2,600 yards in length and at least par 33, and an 18-hole facility must be at least 5,200 yards in length and at least par 66.

Now, a person could make a golf course in his/her back yard. Some people do. A course can be any shape, size, whatever. Nevertheless, to be recognized, it must the parameters described.

Here are some terms that will help you talk like a veteran and impress your friends...

Par 3 Course - - This is a Golf Course which is made up solely of Par 3 holes. Don't confuse this with being easy. Although the mainstream course will be one that is ideal for beginners and juniors, there are some Par 3 Courses (i.e. the Cliffs at Olympic Club in San Francisco) that will be a test for all skill levels.

Executive Course - - This type of course will have some Par 4s or maybe even a Par 5 added into the mix. It offers more variety, but generally falls short of the length and par guidelines to be a Regulation Course. On the surface it might seem that this property has the 'distance challenged' golfer in mind, but it might just be that the geography only allowed a course of the size. In these days of expensive greens fees and with thousands of golf addicts on a tight schedule, a well-manicured Executive Course can be just the ticket.

Championship Course - - Although more of an embodiment than a definition this Golf Course is ready for competition. It has been designed by a reputable architect, is well manicured and you're looking at an overall length of around 6600 yards or more.

GOLF COURSE MANAGEMENT:

Briefly lets go over Golf Course Management. Ultimately it is going to be the Owner of the Property who determines how the Golf Course will be managed. There are some nuances in the details. For example, a Homeowner's Association, may have an influence on the management of a local facility. Our purpose, however, is to bring you up to speed on the basics.

A Private Club is a golf course property that is exclusively used by its Members and their Guests. A Private Party can own this facility, or a Golf Course Management Group which sells memberships (non-proprietary). It can be owned by its own Membership. This is known as a Proprietary Membership.

If the Club has a Proprietary Membership, then it is often self-governing. Usually democratic, a Board of Directors is elected and they develop and maintain the By-Laws and Regulations.

The Members are charged a fee to join (initial deposit), each pays dues on a monthly basis, and when there is major work to be done, they are assessed a share of the total expense. These Clubs are a relatively well-informed group of people, with a collective vested interest in their property. Managed correctly these Clubs can become a home away from home for their Membership.

The Semi-Private Club is trying to achieve the best of both worlds -- the camaraderie, access, and monthly income of a Membership combined with the supplemental revenue of Public Greens Fees. This helps to reduce the cost to the Operator and in turn the Membership. Those who pay greens fee are able to play a top-shelf track that is not impacted by excessive 'open-to-the-public' rounds.

The Public Course is just that, available to all. This category has a broad range of fees and conditions.

Many large cities have their own Golf Course. The Residents of the community (through taxes or bonds) usually foot the bill to build the course. As the Course gains maturity the revenue received from its patrons (greens fees) should allow the course to be self-sufficient. This is known as a Municipal Course. Or, with a blue-collar flare, the Muni.

Most people aren't aware that the Pebble Beach Golf Links is a public golf course. However, it is not a municipal course. It is privately owned and is open to the public. Granted not everyone has the nearly $400 available to pay the greens fee, but nonetheless if there is room in the budget, anyone can play. This type of Public Course is called a Daily Fee.

The Internet is a great source for information about golf courses. Also, many local courses will have periodicals or regional maps available.

Don't be shy, if you want to play a course, review Chapter 5, on golf course reservations. Then give them a call.

Chapter 4

COURTESY TO OTHERS

Emily Post probably played golf. If she didn't, it must have pleased her to know the character, integrity, and behavior of those who play golf for a living. As far as I know, golf is the only sport in which the participants call penalties on themselves. Bear in mind that these athletes are paid based on their performance. Players who do not play well, don't get paid. This isn't like the NBA or the NFL, where players who have a bad week still get a paycheck. One stroke can be the difference in whether or not a player receives a check or the difference between Winner and Runner-up. With bragging rights and a few hundred thousand dollars to separate these positions, that single stroke counts.

Generally speaking, the rest of us who play golf, primarily for entertainment purposes, try to uphold these values for the good of the game. Part of this is evidenced in a respect and a courtesy that we show to our playing partners. We 'honor' the player who plays well on the previous hole. We stand in positions that will not distract those in our group. We are quiet when it is time for someone to hit. It's all wrapped up in a word: Etiquette. The Rules of Golf even dedicate a Section to this topic.

In this chapter, I am going to cover only those issues that will come into play during the normal round. At the same time, there are many 'unwritten' rules when it comes to courtesy. I will go into some of those as well, because I want your conduct to be that of a veteran even if your golf swing appears to be in its infancy.

On the First Tee

For the rounds played outside of a Tournament or Competition, the order of play from the First Tee will typically be chosen in one of two ways. One simple way is to allow the prepared golfer to hit first. This is a good straightforward approach, but often a player does not want to be embarrassed or seem rude by taking the initiative to hit first. So, a pseudo-democratic method has evolved to establish an order. It is quick, decisive and equal opportunity. After any necessary introductions, the players should stand in a fairly structured circle. One of the participants throws a tee into the air in the middle of the group. When the Tee lands it will point at someone or at least nearer to one than the others. This person is First. Throw that Tee up again. Even if it points at the position of the First person it will be closer to one of the remaining Players than another. That person is Second. One more toss and you will have the order.

In competition or Tournament Play, there is a list of players known as a Pairing Sheet. This Sheet designates the Starting Time and the Individual Players broken down into groups. The Order of Play off the First Tee is taken from this Pairing Sheet.

Order of Play for the next Tee

The Rules of Golf cover the order of play based on the scores of the players or 'team' within your Group. For example, after completing the hole, Player A makes a score of 5 and Player B makes a 4. On the next Tee, Player B is the first to hit. This is known as the 'honor'.

During the round you will come across an important issue; what is to be done if there is a tie? If there is a tie (two or more players with the same score on the previous hole), we simply refer to the order from the previous tee. If this also was a tie, you just keep going back, hole by hole, until the tie is broken. So, on the sixth hole Player A makes an 8, Player B makes 6, Player C makes 6, and Player D makes 4. On the previous hole Player A made 8, Player B had a 7, Player C made a 5, and Player D made 4. What is the order of play on the seventh hole? Player D had the 'honor' (with the lowest score), next up is Player C (the tie with player B was broken with the score of 5 on the previous hole), followed by Player B and then Player A, (who on this hole had the highest score). *Refer to Rules of Golf; Rule 10*

In another chapter (Chapter 10) I will cover a series of steps or 'Routine' that veteran players will repeat prior to hitting each shot. For now, lets move on...

ORDER OF PLAY

		Hole 1	Hole 2	Hole 3	Hole 4	Hole 5	Hole 6	ORDER OF PLAY for Hole 7
PLAYER A	score	3	4	5	6	8	8	FOURTH
PLAYER B	score	6	5	4	3	7	6	THIRD
PLAYER C	score	3	3	3	4	5	6	SECOND
PLAYER D	score	8	9	9	7	4	4	FIRST

Ready Golf on the Tee

I need to qualify each of the following scenarios by stating that the most important courtesy that you can show the players in your Group and those who follow you on the Golf Course is to play at a good pace. Honors, Order of Play, Beverage Carts, all of these things take a back seat to Pace of Play. Although it's not in the Rules of Golf, if our Group is out of position (the group in front of you is two shots away or too much time has elapsed in your round) then, whoever is ready should play the next shot. On the Tee, if you get there first, hit it. In the fairway, if it is safe, hit it. You should communicate this with your Group. You don't want to offend anyone or catch him or her off guard. This is also a good subtle way to inform someone, if they are not aware of the group's position. The phrase is "lets play Ready Golf". When you catch up, go back to the 'Honor' system.

In the Fairway

Believe it or not, maneuvering in the Fairway is somewhat of an art. You are trying to juggle two things. On the one hand you are trying to mentally prepare for the next shot and put yourself in a position to hit. On the other hand you are trying to avoid being killed by another player and not distract someone.

After everyone has hit their first shot, or 'Tee Shot', your Golf Club is returned to the Golf Bag and you are on your way. If you are walking, it is very simple, after a few steps through the grass with one of your playing partners; you change your heading and take a direct route toward your golf ball. In a Cart, the Driver should accelerate down the Cart Path until the appropriate time to drive on the grass and toward his/her ball (see Chapter 6 on Golf Carts). Although this is an opportunity to be social, remember that Pace of Play is the primary objective. Again, the advanced player does not care about your skill level. A horrible player, who plays quickly, is much more appealing than the 'wanna-be' player who proves ineptitude through slow play. So, say a few words, break the ice, and make sure that you have located your golf ball. Next, position your self physically and prepare yourself mentally for your next shot.

Order of Play in the Fairway

The player whose ball is furthest from the hole plays first. This doesn't mean that the other players just hang out and watch. If the others waited and watched each time another played his/her shot, it would take all day. While the other golfer is playing his or her shot, you should move as near to your golf ball as possible without being a distraction or putting yourself in harm's way.

At this point, you are able to begin gathering the information that you need to hit your next shot. This inner monologue will sound like this; How far am I from the hole? Is this next shot uphill or downhill? Do I feel or see any wind? How is my 'lie', will I be able to hit the ball cleanly?

All of these answers will point you to a choice. This is the shot I choose to hit and this is the club that I choose to use. Locate the club, pull it from your bag and be ready to go. When your ball is furthest from the hole, it is your turn. *Refer to Rules of Golf: Rule 10*

Ready Golf on the Fairway

When your Group is on time and in position relative to the other Groups on the Course, this process can be somewhat rhythmical. Player A hits, then Player B, Player C, etc. However, if the Group is behind or out of position, dispense with some of the formality and just hit the ball when you are ready. Of course, you would never want to distract someone or put them in an awkward position, but if it is safe and would not bother anyone, you should hit to speed things up. Communicate with your Group. "Hey, we're a little behind, I'll go over and hit my shot and meet up with you later." That's impressive.

Around the Putting Green

Here is a scenario. Your ball is in some longer grass, just off the putting surface, 20' away from the hole. A playing partner is on the Green with about a 40' putt. The average player will give himself or herself away when they expect the golfer with the shorter shot to play. It doesn't matter whether someone is on or off of the Putting Green, the player whose ball is farther from the hole, is next to play.

You will ask this question throughout the round, but most of the time you will hear it around the Green; 'who's away?' This is as simple as it sounds. You just want to make sure everyone is on the same page for the order of play.

There will be situations, however, in which playing 'out of order' might be better. This is a mindset to have in order to keep things moving along. For those of us playing for 'entertainment only' purposes, there is no problem mixing up the order a bit.

You should just communicate with the players in your group. The phrase you're looking for is, "I'll go ahead and come up," or, "Why don't you go ahead and come up?" It means that you are going to hit your ball 'up' onto the green. Even if the ball goes downhill, we still use the word 'up'. This will let the group know that the formalities have been bypassed for either convenience or pace of play.

On the Putting Green

Many of the issues are the same here as on the Fairway, but due to proximity, are now explained in greater detail. The furthest from the hole plays first. You should be thinking about your putt before you hit it.

Do not stand in a position that could distract the player who is putting or on the 'line' of their putt. The best spot to stand is either directly behind or directly in front of the player who is putting and a good twenty or more feet away. Never, ever stand to the side of the Player who is about to Putt. This would place you on an extension of their 'line.'

When the person is about to hit their Putt, they bend over. Anything that is in front or behind them cannot be seen. However, when you bend over to hit a Putt, your eyes still pick up things to each side. Not only is this distracting, but it can seem downright tacky. This is a way that some players will try to view another's shot and gain an advantage. Don't get me wrong, there is a place for this knowledge. In fact, we have a phrase 'going to school' on a putt.

After someone hits his or her putt, then you can move over and take a look at how the putt rolls. This just needs to be much more subtle than standing on the line of someone's Putt to gain an edge.

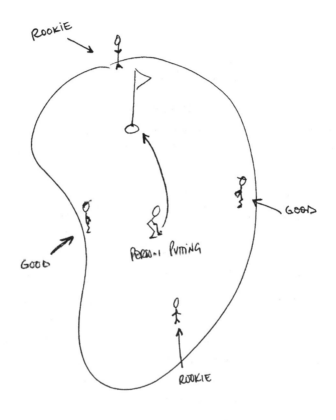

ROOKIE

GOOD

GOOD

PERSON PUTTING

ROOKIE

WHERE TO STAND WHEN OTHERS ARE PUTTING

What is the 'line' of a Putt?

Very few portions of a Putting Green will be perfectly level. So, when you hit a Putt, the ball often does not roll straight. This path of travel between the ball and the hole is simply called, the Line.

Prior to hitting a putt, you want to establish two things. One, determine how hard do you have to hit it. Two, you need to decide which path you would like the ball to take. Keep this in mind; the speed of the ball will affect the amount of break. A ball that rolls quickly will be less susceptible to the slope. However, you don't want to hit the ball so hard that your next putt becomes a problem.

Have you ever walked in a room, looked up at the wall, and noticed that one of the pictures isn't level? Perhaps you have worked on a project and realized the borders or the parameters of the object were not quite right? Some people are aware of the lie of the land and others are not. This ability to survey your environment will come in very handy when it is time to putt. Our ability to 'read' or see these undulations is very valuable.

Of course, the shorter the put t, the less opportunity for the lie of the land and gravity to take effect on a rolling ball. On longer distances, there can be large amounts of what we call 'break', or the amount of movement that a ball will turn during the course of the putt.

The comments that you will hear on the putting green will be things like, "How much do you think this is going to break?" and "Boy, that was a good read, too bad I hit it through the break."

You should never step on someone else's line. Depending on the ground conditions, a footprint might stay for several minutes which could cause a rolling golf ball to change directions. This is not good. As a result, it is normal to hear a lot of chatter on the Green about the Lines. "Hey, where is everybody at?" "Is this your mark here?" And the closer you get to the hole (after your first putt) the more careful that you have to be.

You must be aware of the general location of the other player's line at all times.

This is why players will sometimes assume an awkward stance near the hole. They are trying to hit their Putt without stepping on the line of another Putt. They could, however, choose to wait. *Refer to Rules of Golf: Section I Etiquette*

Marking your Ball

Under normal circumstances, you are not allowed to 'lift' the ball without penalty, until the ball has reached the Putting Green. If there is mud or grass on the ball, that's just the way it goes. You play it. Once the ball has come to rest on the Green, you may 'lift' the ball. At this point, you may clean it, rub it, give it positive affirmation, and then snuggle it away in your pocket.

Marking the ball is done by placing a 'coin or other similar object' (Rule 20) immediately behind the ball. So, keeping the ball between yourself and the hole, put the coin on the ground directly behind the ball. This maneuver should take place in two pieces; one to place coin and one to pick up the ball. A sign of a novice is the attempt to make this happen in one motion. In fact, many will break the rule by first moving the ball and then replacing it with a coin. Don't worry, get the coin down first. The rules even provide for a ball that is moved in this process. The ball is simply replaced without penalty.

Now, you may pick up or 'lift' the ball. When it is your turn, keeping the coin between yourself and the hole, place the ball directly in front of the coin. The ball is in play. Finally, pick up the coin. *Refer to Rules of Golf: Rule 20*

Let me give you a Veteran move. I've gone over the importance of avoiding an impression on the line of a putt. How much more important is the problem of a coin in the path of someone's golf ball? Here is what you do. First ask the potential victim if the coin is in the way. It goes something like this, "Is this coin okay here?" Obviously, if the other player does not object, you just leave it where it is. However, if it does bother the player, then you need to move it.

Before we move the ball, there is a follow-up question. Knowing that we are not perfect, when a player putts, he or she may miss the intended Line. The better players will know which side of the line to hedge their bet in the event of a miss. So, the coin needs to be moved to the correct side -- the side of the Line the ball will not roll on. This is often noted by the topography. You either move the coin 'up' or 'down'. If the coin is to be moved 'up' then we move it in the direction of higher ground (uphill) and if the coin is to be moved 'down' then we move it toward lower ground (downhill).

This is how it's done. Holding the Putter in one hand, place the Putter Head on the ground with the very end of the Putter Head touching the edge of the coin. To ensure that the angle of your putter head is the same when you replace the mark, pick out an object in the background (trees work real well). Imagine a line between the object and your ball. Place the putter head on this imaginary line. This will give you a reference point for your Putter Head when the coin is returned to its original position. The coin is then lifted and placed on the other end of the Putter Head. The coin is now one clubhead length away from its original location. In most cases your job is done, walk away. Occasionally, to make the Player more comfortable, you might need to move it further. Just repeat the process.

Once that player has putted, use the same procedure to put the coin back in its original position. Do that as soon as possible. Even the players on Tour forget sometimes and you will receive a penalty if you hit the next putt from anywhere other than its original location. *Rules of Golf: Rule 18*

The Flagstick

A ball that begins on the Putting Green is not supposed to hit the Flagstick. Presumably, the Flagstick could be used as a 'backstop' for the ball. So, when all of the Players in the group have their ball on the Green and can see the hole, you just take out the Flag and set it down away from play.

What do you do if a player's ball is on the green, but the hole cannot be seen very well, if at all? If the player chooses to keep the flag in the hole, and then proceeds hit the flagstick with a well-aimed putt, he/she will be penalized. If you take the flag out, the hole cannot be seen. Our duty is to hold the Flagstick for the player until the putt has been hit. When the ball is on its way to the hole, you pull the Flagstick out. Were the ball to hit the hole, it will not hit the Flagstick. This is known as 'tending' the flag, which I will cover in a moment.

When your shot begins with the ball on the putting green, it is a penalty if the ball hits the flagstick. When your ball is 'off' the putting (no part of the ball touches the putting surface) there is no penalty for hitting the flagstick. You have the option of taking the flagstick out of the hole, having the flagstick tended, or leaving the flagstick in the hole. Lets take a moment and discuss the choice of leaving the Flagstick 'in' or taking the Flagstick 'out' option.

Conventional wisdom says that when a ball hits the pin, it only helps the bad shot (by decreasing its speed). The good shot (in the center) hits the Flag and stays out. Also for the good shot (good line, good speed) the pin takes up a certain amount of space (volume) of the hole, which could prevent the ball from going in. So, if you are comfortable with the speed and line, take the flag out. When you are unsure, leave the flag in, it may help a shot that is hit too hard.

Taking the flagstick out, or leaving it in, is a simple communication thing. If a player wants the flag 'out', he/she can either take it out himself or ask for another player to take it out. Also, the flagstick may be taken out of the hole for someone whose ball has not reached the green if they feel that the flagstick might hurt his or her chances. If a player would rather leave the flagstick in the hole, we simply leave it alone and find a good spot to stand.

Okay, back to our regularly scheduled programming. When each player in the group has a ball on the Putting Green, take a mental survey. Is there anyone who might not be able to see the hole from where there ball is? If so, just ask. It will sound like this, "Do you (anyone) need the flag (pin)?" On the Tour this is the responsibility of the Player whose ball is on the Green first. Virtually none of the players in your group with will know this. So, usually the person who is closest to the hole will take the initiative. If everyone can see, you pull the Flag out (remember the Lines) and place it away from any action. *Refer to Rules of Golf: Rule 17*

Tending the Flag

Sometimes, a player will respond with 'would you mind tending that for me?' In this instance, take your position an arms length from the Flagstick. Be aware of the Lines of the other players and the shadows that you might cast on the line of the player who is about to Putt. With the Flagstick held at arms length, stand motionless until the Putt has been hit. Once the ball is on its way, gently pull the Flag out and wait for the ball to arrive. Does anyone else need the Flag? If so, replace the Flagstick and repeat the process.

When everyone can see the hole set the Flag down in a spot where it will not be in play. When everyone has completed the hole, replace the flag for the last time and you're off to the next hole.

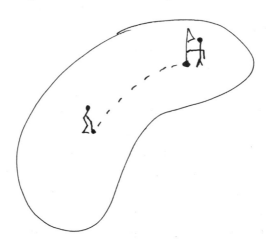

TEND THE FLAG AT ARM'S LENGTH...
... CHOOSE TO STAND IN A LOCATION THAT WILL NOT CAST SHADOWS ON THE PLAYER'S LINE.

Sounds on the Course

Birds, squirrels running up a tree, a well struck tee shot, those are acceptable sounds on the golf course. Our ears enjoy nature.

Cell phones ringing, the warning buzzer of a golf cart in reverse, someone coughing during your golf swing, these are unacceptable sounds on the course.

When someone is about to play we must do everything in our power to create a quiet environment. This is a moment in time when you need to make sure that you're not even breathing too loud.

Before and after the golfer hits the ball, you can talk, blow bubbles, or pull a golf club from your bag, whatever. There is freedom to walk around, smell the roses, and relax.

As soon as it is time for a player to swing, you must stop everything. There is a grey area, but this quiet period begins as the player assumes their address position.

Players will make a few practice swings before they move close enough to the ball to hit it. When they start to put themselves in a position to make a stroke, everything that you are doing needs to stop.

If you are taking a club out of your bag, stop. Just hold it in the air for a moment if you have to. If you are conversing with another player in the group, hold that thought. It will only take a couple of seconds and you can go right back to what you were doing.

Before you operate a golf cart, take a look around you. Make sure that no one is in the middle of hitting the ball. The brake release, or the warning sound of a cart in reverse gear, are likely to earn you a dirty look if engaged at the wrong time.

Old golf courses may have tees and greens that are very close together. So, before you hit, take a look around. If you see a person leaning over a putt, it is a good idea to wait and hit your tee shot in a moment or two.

The golf course, however, doesn't have to be a library. When you, or someone in your group sinks a long putt, or hits a ball close to the pin, give a good hoot or holler. Follow this up with a golfers high-five.

Courtesy is the word. The golf course is not a monastery. There will be loud moments and quiet times. The objective is to make sure that you are participating in the correct activity at the correct time.

Mutterings

The bottom line is a concern for others. Be aware of the play of your Group and your relationship on the course to other Groups. Just as in life off the course, if you put a premium on respecting those around you, people of quality will respect you.

Throughout your round, feel free to encourage others. When someone hits a good shot, tell him or her. Phrases like 'nice one', 'good try', or the simple 'golf shot' should ring out. At the same time, the best thing to do in the event of a poor shot is to not say a word unless you are very skilled in diplomacy.

In many Groups across the Country the players have become so familiar with each other that like your family, you enjoy giving them a bad time when they miss a shot that could have gone well. A ball traveling toward the sand is encouraged to 'bury', or a shot that is traveling too far is told to 'get outta here'. My wife's initiation to golf was in just such a group of guys.

A good friend of mine and I were playing in a Northern California PGA team event several years ago. My wife, indoctrinated by my peers, but still new to the game, came along and was observing. One of our Opponents was on the Tee and hit a ball that had no chance of landing on the Golf Course. Not knowing that we had just met these guys and wanting to participate in the group, she naturally exclaimed,

"See ya!" There was no way for my partner and I to explain, so we kept it to ourselves and chuckled down the fairway. Ironically, this seemed to break the ice and soon all of us were like old friends. Maybe they did the same thing back home.

Chapter 5

WITHOUT RESERVATIONS

More and more services in the Golf Business, as well as other industries, have become automated. A phone call is placed to reserve a Starting Time for a round of golf. Rather than a personal greeting, the caller is often engaged by a recording and a list of options. Staff in the Golf Shop receive the comment, 'I'd rather talk to a human.' In fact, people will make a reservation over an automated system and then call the Golf Shop to confirm.

Another modern 'convenience' for the Golf Industry is the use of a 21st century Global Positioning System (GPS). GPS is a Satellite based locator. Objects that are online with the system can be located virtually anywhere in the world. This can assist golf courses in many ways, and today, a practical benefit is the ability to inform a Golfer how far he/she is from the intended target (yardage). Using the GPS data, a golfer will know how far his/her golf cart is from another object on the grid. Most of the time this is the flagstick.

Now this same 'someone', who doesn't trust the Automated Phone Reservation System, is on the Golf Course trying to get yardage information. Even though this is my home course and I know the exact distance to the flagstick, the golfer will not ask me. Knowing that the information is available from the GPS, he/she will ask, 'What does the Cart say?', preferring to get information from the machine. A person could even *offer* the correct yardage and it would not be enough. There would be doubt, due to a possibility of human error.

This is puzzling to me, because that same person who is reluctant to make a starting time via the machine is now trusting the machine over a person due to the prospect of human error.

As we all know, the machine is more trustworthy -- until we want to make a Reservation. Human nature is an amazing thing.

Making a Starting Time is very similar to making any other reservation, although in the Golf Business we don't often use the word 'reservation'. It is known as a Starting Time or a Tee Time. By the way, don't use the single word 'Tee' or the phrase 'Tee-off' when speaking of a starting time.

You need to have your information ready before you make that call; What day do you want to play? What time do you want to play? How many players do you have? If you have questions about directions, food service, etc. these answers may very well be automated also. Let your fingers do the walking and by the way, have a Credit Card number handy.

With many automated systems a Credit Card number is required to make a reservation. An amount does not get charged to your account. The credit card number is just held in the system until the day of play. When you arrive at the course you can choose to pay however you prefer. If you fail to appear for your Starting Time this credit card will typically be charged a 'No-Show Fee' and the system will make a note that you bailed.

There still are some Golf Shops that actually answer the phone. If this happens, have your questions ready and to the point. If you are not prepared or haven't thought the whole thing through, the phone call can go sideways real fast. You would not believe how some of these conversations go. What you're about to read is true; the names have been changed to protect the guilty.

"Thank you for calling the Wolsner Golf Course. This is John. May I help you?"

"What's the earliest starting time you have on Friday?"

"How's seven o'clock?'

"Oh, gee, do you have anything later?"

If you don't want the earliest time, don't ask for it. Just tell the person what you want, they will do their best to reserve the time for you.

Golf Courses have intervals between Starting Times. These intervals will vary from property to property. Some courses have six or seven minutes between groups. Others allow up to fifteen minutes between groups. This means that when you ask for a Starting Time that is generally going to be on the hour (10:00 am), the response will be some fraction of an hour (10:07 am).

Here's another true story.

"Thank you for calling the Mootser Golf Course. This is John. May I help you?"

"Hi, do you have anything on Thursday around 10:00 am?"

"How's 10:10 am?"

"Oh, gee, that's going to be too late."

How can a ten-minute variable be the deciding factor with an event that will take at least five hours to complete? Consider all of the factors influencing that day and that round of golf. The weather, the pace of play on the golf course, a possible delay in the starting time, driving time to and from the golf course, and traffic on the roads, are all issues that will have an impact on the length of time spent at a golf course. The most accurate guesses would have to have a thirty-minute tolerance.

Imagine making a dinner reservation at a restaurant. Your request was 6:00 pm. However, the hostess informed you that 6:10pm was the first availability. Would that be enough to skip dinner or search for the restaurant that was able to get you in a 5:58 pm?

There are many of these phone call stories that we could pass along and what is remarkable is that these are not ice-cube in hell scenarios. The unique calls haven't been included. These happen often enough that they continue to baffle me. Here is one more model call. It is cited only because it is repeated several times, everyday at every Golf Shop.

"Thank you for calling the Yugi Golf Course. This is John. May I help you?"

"Hey, do you have anything on Saturday at 10:00 am?"

"No, the first available starting time that I have on Saturday is at 2:00 pm."

'Nothing earlier, huh?"

This can cross industry lines. Robert Erler and I worked together for some years at a Golf Course in Livermore. His daughter asked for tickets to a concert at the Arena. Dutifully, he did some research and phoned to make the purchase.

Here is how his conversation went.

'Thank you for calling the Widget Ticket Agency'

'Hey, I would like to buy four tickets in Section 24, right in the middle.'

'Sorry, the best that we have left is Section 43 on the end.'

'Nothing near Section 24, huh?'

We both got a good laugh out of that one.

When you call for a starting time and it's not available, just bite your tongue. Many 'But, if I' and 'If you could just' phrases will come to mind. It will be tempting, but don't do it.

This comes back to where we started. Human nature. The person in the Golf Shop is not holding back information. Additional questioning will not result in a different answer. You get the idea though. Have your information together and accept what the attendant tells you. Remember, he/she is on your side.

Chapter 6

DRIVING YOU CRAZY

Drivers of golf carts must adhere to certain regulations at each golf course. Most rules are based in common sense. Other guidelines may be conditional, based on weather, or created specifically for a unique layout. Taking little for granted, courses often post signs and give verbal instructions.

Many properties today have particular areas of the course that are protected from motorized carts. One of these is known as an 'Environmentally Sensitive Area'. Seasonally, this might appear as creeks with lush, spring greenery or as summer hillsides covered with hay.

These areas of unmaintained or 'native' grasses are not only identified on the scorecards and on the cart message holder, but at our golf course the Starter on the first hole announces the condition to all groups. However, cart drivers can develop amnesia, especially when it means that there is a long walk to search for an errant golf ball.

Just such a situation required one of our golf course Marshals to remind a golf cart driver that the sign in the cart and the Starter on the first tee asked him to not drive in the Native Grass. The man replied, "but I'm not driving through any native grass, I'm just driving through this dead s#@t!'

There are many things you need to know about something as simple as a golf cart. My priority is to give you sufficient information so that you can conduct yourself as if you are a veteran of the game and an experienced driver of a golf cart. Safety is a concern as well, but we will take care of your ego first.

LOADING THE BAG -- Each golf course property will vary in its level of service. As is everything else in life, you get what you pay for. Some will have an Attendant that will whisk your golf bag from your trunk while you and your car pause near the Clubhouse entrance. Others will require you to handle your own bag until it is firmly fastened on the cart. The following scenario will assume the lease amount of assistance. If you get some help, it will be that much better.

Imagine that you have dropped off your golf bag at the 'Bag Drop' that is usually located next to a curb near the Clubhouse. You park the car and enter the Pro Shop. After you have paid your greens fees, make your way to the Cart Staging area. Look for a significant number of Golf Carts arranged in rows. They should be noticeable. If it is not obvious, this is a question that you should ask one of the Service Staff. Where are your golf carts located?

After signing the obligatory 'release of liability' form, the first order of business is to position your bag on the cart. At the rear of the cart there is a harness and strap near the back of the seat. There will also be a large tray at the base, near the rear bumper. The bag will go here. Hold on a minute, this is a good time to determine who would like to drive. The Driver's bag goes to the left (on the Driver's side) and the 'passenger's' bag will go on the right.

Whether you place your own golf bag or an attendant will load it for you, you **must** verify that the bag is secure. Seems simple, but considering the investment in your equipment, you don't want to take this for granted.

There is a strap in the center of the harness that works like a belt. Move the belt around your bag (possible through the handle of the bag) and into a plastic buckle on the outside of the harness. Press the buckle down tight. Give the belt a good tug. Make sure that it is taut and the bag is secure. A good way to get your round off to a rookie start is to have your bag fall off of the back of the cart. If I had a dollar for every time....

GOLF CART OPERATION:

Turn the Cart On -- Similar to a car, the first objective is to make sure the vehicle is turned on. You probably won't hear anything, as most golf carts have electric motors. Locate the key and verify that it is in the 'ON' position.

Gears -- Golf Carts do not have multiple gears. The cart is either in Forward or Reverse. Each carts has a Forward/Reverse Switch. This is often located on the 'dashboard' of the cart or on a panel beneath the seat next to the floor board. You should find the cart staged in Forward and when necessary a switch can be made to 'Reverse'. When in 'Reverse', a really annoying, warning buzzer will sound. Upon completing your maneuver, return the switch to forward and the noise will stop.

Stop 'n Go -- In order to move or stop the vehicle there are only two pedals. One is the *accelerator* and the other is the brake. The brake pedal, however, has two parts. The top portion is the parking *brake* or emergency brake. When you push on it, a clicking sound can be heard, and the pedal should stay depressed. This means that the brake is locked in place. Go ahead an push this down every time that you park the cart. Let me clarify, this is for parking, not for reducing speed.

For slowing the cart, you will use the lower portion of the pedal. Please don't push the top portion of the pedal to slow the cart. It will lock the brake and send your passenger headlong through the window. So, use the lower part the pedal to slow down and stop. Once you have stopped the cart, give the top part a good shove to lock the emergency brake in place.

The *emergency brake* can be released by using one of two methods; either push the lower part of the pedal until the upper part unlocks, or simply push the accelerator. The accelerator is designed to release the brake under normal driving conditions, if necessary. Of course, when you use the accelerator to release the brake, the cart may jolt forward on you a little bit. This doesn't really matter when your on the open road, but in tight quarters, you will need to be very careful. Just tap the accelerator enough to release the brake and not leap into the cart in front of you. On the course, you can simply depress the accelerator and the brake will release automatically and you will be on your way.

When you are close to objects or people, or you want to maintain control of the brake, release the parking brake by pushing the bottom portion of the pedal. This will unlock the brake, but you will still have control of the brake. (On occasion this mechanism will stick and it will be difficult to release the brake. When this happens, just tap the accelerator.)

DRIVING TO THE PRACTICE RANGE:

When you ride to the Driving Range to hit a few balls before you play, look around. Use discretion as your guide. Is there a specific area for Parking Carts? If you run out of Cart Path, park your cart and walk the rest the way. Think of how you are going to get out (and to the First Tee) before you park. Its really embarrassing to pin yourself in and have to implement the 'three point turn' half a dozen times.

DRIVING ON THE COURSE:

The Shop Personnel, Cart Attendant or Starter should inform you of the Cart Rules before you begin play. Often there is a message holder in the Golf Cart stating certain cart rules. Essentially, there are two main categories of golf course access during a round of golf; 'Carts on Path Only' or the '90° Rule'.

If the Golf Carts are restricted to the paths or as commonly known, 'Cart Path Only', then things are pretty simple. The paved area prepared for the Golf Cart is called the Cart Path. Your golf cart must remain on this path at all times. Depending on the property, and the season, golf carts may be restricted to this path throughout the round. Otherwise, Golf Carts are allowed to be taken on to the course.

When golf carts are allowed to be driven on the course, there is a procedure, this is not a free for all. Carts are to be driven using the '90° Rule.' That's 90 degrees, not 90 percent. This means that, generally speaking, we are to drive golf carts at 90° angles in relationship to the cart path. Of course, it isn't possible to do this perfectly, 100% of the time. It is a guideline that we observe in order to reduce the impact that golf carts may have on the course.

In concept, the golf cart is to be driven on the path until you reach a point that is perpendicular to the ball. At that point, you will turn right or left (depending on the relation of the ball and the cart path) and continue on the grass toward your ball. Park the cart a safe distance behind the ball and prepare to hit your shot. After the ball has been hit, get back in the cart and return directly to the cart path. Once you are back on the path, repeat the process. Here is a diagram of how this might look.

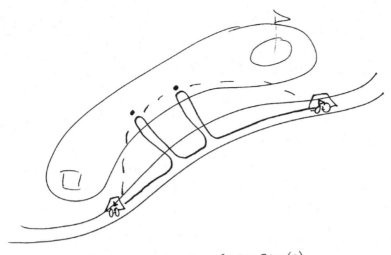

- BLACK DOT IS THE GOLF BALL(S)
- — SOLID LINE IS THE CORRECT 90° PATTERN
- --- HASH MARKS ARE THE ROOKIE MANEUVER

To protect the areas around the putting greens, there will be signs or stakes or areas that are 'roped off'. If you do not locate or recognize these, conventional wisdom would have us stay at least thirty yards away from Greens and Tees. You should continue this procedure until you are too close to the putting green to drive on the grass.

This basic information is critical to your success driving the cart, but remember that the purpose of this book is more than a basic education. Our goal is to help you behave like a veteran even if you don't have the game. As such, even with something straight forward as 'Cart Paths Only' there are some subtle maneuvers that you can make to help you appear as the veteran. In time, you will see that these are just common sense, but early in your 'career' you need a 'cheat sheet,' so lets go through a few on course tips.

Driving near tees and fairways --

- At the first tee (and subsequent tees), park toward the front of the teeing ground to allow others who are playing with you to park next to the tee as well.

- Always stay to the side of the Cart Path when you park. This allows others (maintenance, marshals, players in your group) driving vehicles to get by.

- Park in a position that allows you to walk forward after you hit your shot. We never want to walk backward or drive away from the hole. So, when you get to your ball, park the cart even or slightly ahead of the ball position. This way when you are done hitting your shot, you can move forward.

- Be very aware of signage that restricts Golf Carts from certain areas, specifically around Greens and Tees.

- There is usually a roped off zone around the Greens or a distance noted on Scorecard or Golf Cart that informs one to keep the Cart away from areas close to the Greens.

- If you leave the Path to hit your shot and your partner's ball is ten yards in front of you, don't go directly back to the path. Move the cart forward a few yards if you're really lazy. Or, ideally, just keep the Cart where it is. Park the cart in a position that serves both players. After you both hit take the Cart back to the Path and proceed.

- How far can you drive ahead without being in the way?? This is the question that you should ask yourself every time you drive near the fairway.

PARKING THE CART NEAR BUNKERS ...

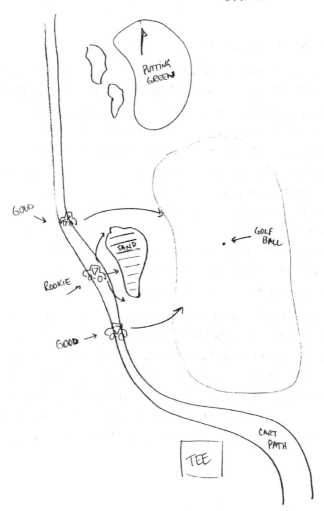

Driving Near the Green --

- When parking around the Green, park as near to the next hole as possible. Some courses will have prepared a place for Carts to park near the Green, at others it is much more random. But if given the choice, park as near to the next Tee as possible. This way you are already walking forward and its somewhat of a rookie move to have to get into your cart move it just a few paces down the road. Its much easier to put your Putter into your bag and get your club for the next Tee than having to adjust the position of your Cart. In fact, sometimes the best thing to do is to park at the next tee. Especially, if your ball is on the Green and the only Club that you will need is your putter. Ask your partner what Club they need and bring it along.

- When near the Green, but this can apply elsewhere, don't park in a place that puts a bunker between you and where you are going. Try not to park the Cart in a location that will require you to walk around something (this could be water also) to get to your ball. Park either at the beginning or the end of the bunker to give you a straight path to your ball. Find the spot that is beyond the ball and has a direct line to the Cart.

A Coordinated Effort --

Go Team....when you have more than one rider in the cart, communication will go a long way in making the round more enjoyable for you and those playing behind you. Feel free to ask questions of your partner and also let them know what you are doing.

Case in point, sometimes it is actually a shorter walk directly to the Green or your next shot, rather than walking back to the cart, exchanging clubs, moving the cart and then walking back to the ball. In this situation, just inform your partner that you are going to walk and if necessary, ask them to get a Golf Club for you. On the next hole, you might do the same for them.

This is a good foundation for the operation of a Golf Cart and with this information you are way ahead of the pack when it comes to looking like a pro. Now you just need to do it often enough that you have confidence in what you are doing. Along the way, if you screw up and park the cart in place that is ground zero for your partners next shot or you accidentally drive it into the Lake on the 9th hole (don't laugh its been done), just throw out a quick 'sorry'. Like everything else in life, people will only remember if you don't apologize.

Chapter 7

WHAT'S IN YOUR BAG?

One summer, I had the opportunity to instruct a group that included some local elementary school teachers. From what I recall it was week #2 when one of these educators looked at me and asked, "What's a 'wwhhu'?"

"A what?" I queried. In earnest, she described it again, "I have a 'wwhhu'." For what must have seemed like minutes, I paused to sort through my mental database. Soon, she produced her golf club that had a 'W' on the end of it.

Numbers are used to identify some golf clubs, while others have names. It isn't practical for the equipment manufacturers to spell out the entire name on the end of a golf club. Instead there is often a large and legible initial or abbreviation stamped on the club.

It didn't come to me until I saw the evidence. She was holding a 'Wedge'. We soon discovered that there were other letters lurking on a variety of clubs in her golf bag. A 'Sand wedge' is typically stamped with an 'S' and a 'Lob wedge' would be stamped with an 'L.' These clubs would become known as a 'Ssss' and 'Llll.'

HOW MANY DO YOU NEED?

A hundred years ago there were no regulations on the number of golf clubs that a player could use during the round. Some competitors would have near forty clubheads peeking out of the top of their bag. (Of course, it was the caddy that had to carry it.) This made things a little easier for some players, because it required less skill. So, in the late 1930's the Rules of Golf contained a new rule limiting each set to a maximum of fourteen.

Depending upon your ambition, you may not even have fourteen clubs in your bag. Shoot, I enjoy a good walk on the course, but I would rather not pack my bag. When I have to carry my bag, I lighten my load and deposit a few clubs in the trunk of the car. Of course, there is no minimum, but realistically you will need at least five or six clubs to play on the course. With one of the woods, three of the irons and a putter, you can play golf.

Although there will be circumstances in which you might choose to limit yourself to certain number of clubs, ultimately you will need to fill the golf bag with the maximum. A player can 'get by' with less, but in doing this, the game becomes more difficult. You could dig a hole using only a pole, but that shovel would come in really handy. The game is challenging enough, so to have less than the maximum is selling us short.

WHAT DO THEY DO?

Categorically, we have woods, irons, and a putter. Here is how you will use them;

Woods: These are the longest golf clubs in the bag. When struck with a decent swing, they will cause the ball to travel farther then your irons. The caveat is that the club that will produce the greater distance is also the most challenging to hit solid and to control. (See Chapter 16: Equipment)

Before the 20th Century, golf clubs were given names. To name a few, clubs that were previously identified as Spoon, Mashie, or Niblick, made a conversion to numbers. These numbers are still used today. In fact, we have graduated to a new level of detail by designating some golf clubs by their degrees of loft. This is the number of degrees of angle on the face of the club relative to top dead center. Each tick off center, or degree, is measured and noted to identify the club.

LOFT ANGLE ILLUSTRATION - DEGREES

On average drivers measure from around..... 7° to 12°

What used to be called a#2 wood is........... 12° to 13°

#3 wood .... 13° to 16°

#4 wood .... 18° to 20°

#5 wood .... 22° +/-

#7 wood .... 24° +/-

Driver: A Driver should be used almost exclusively off the Tee. There are some very skilled players who will try the Driver from the fairway, if their ball is in a very favorable situation. This is known as 'hitting it off the deck.' For most of us, we should limit the Driver's use to the Tee.

Fairway Woods: With the exception of the Driver, the rest of the woods are known as Fairway Woods. (Yes, they're metal -- please refer to Chapter 16). This does not mean that they cannot be hit off the Tee; it is simply not their primary purpose. The shape of the head, the loft, and the way that weight is distributed inside the head make it easier to get the ball airborne from the ground

The #3 wood has a smaller head than a driver, has more degrees of loft, and a rounded sole for use from the fairway At the same time, the length of the golf club allows it to be used as a 'driver' if necessary. It can be used in place of the Driver for shorter holes, or as I often recommend, it can replace the Driver any time that it makes you feel more comfortable. Let's face it, that Driver can be intimidating. For many players, a lot of time and golf balls have been sacrificed at the ego alter of the Driver.

You would rather find a drive (hit with a #3 wood) that is 20 - 30 yards short of your maximum distance (hit with the Driver), than try for maximum distance and begin the search through the tundra for your golf ball. Not to mention the price of golf balls these days.

Categorized as 'trouble clubs' the #5 and #7 are a good choice when hitting out of longer grass or when you need to get more height on the shot. The club heads are even smaller, with more loft, and progressively shorter shafts.

Even when you're not in 'trouble' these clubs can be used from the fairway or off the tee when you are looking for a more specific distance. Relative to the long irons (#2, #3, #4 iron), the heads are larger, and it is easier to get the ball in the air. So, you might choose these as a replacement for the irons when longer shots remain on Par-4's or for Tee shots on Par-3's.

Irons: While the woods are primarily used to 'advance' the ball, the Irons are to be more of a precision instrument. You are looking for accuracy *and* consistency in distance.

Each iron has a different length and a different loft. In a typical set, the length will be reduced by 1/2" per club from the longest to the shortest. Also, the amount of loft will increase progressively (between 2°-4° per club) from the longer clubs to the shorter clubs. For example, a #9 iron would be 1/2" shorter and have 4° more loft than the #8 iron of the same set. When you do the math, similar swings will produce a higher, but shorter shot with the #9 iron. The easiest way to remember this is that the higher number on the club, the higher the ball flight and in turn a shorter shot. Depending upon the player, this difference between clubs will be about 5 - 10 yards.

HOW FAR SHOULD THEY GO?

On the golf course, these measurements and distances will be very important. The scorecards note overall distance, and there are markers on the golf course to inform you how far you are from your intended target. You need to know the approximate distance that a ball will fly when hit with a certain club. Case in point, if you have 100 yards remaining to the flagstick or green, you need to know which club should be used to hit the ball 100 yards.

First, take a mid-range club like a #5 or #7 iron. Find a place that you can hit a few shots and measure their distance. Frankly the driving range is not your best option. Range balls often do not travel as far as balls sold over the counter and it is difficult to gauge the distance from the tee. If possible, find a practice area or go to the golf course at a time when you have the opportunity to hit two or three balls. A Par-3 where you can reach the green with one swing is perfect. (Note: some golf courses may prohibit playing more than one ball, if this is the case, please respect the regulation)

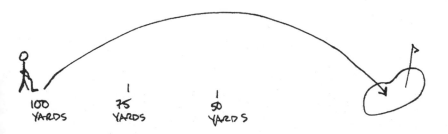

100 YARDS   75 YARDS   50 YARDS

Once you have a good idea about the distance for this club, it will be used as a basis for the other clubs. Heck, if you have the time and resources, measure them all. For most of us, we will use that measurement, then subtract or add that 5 – 10 yards to come up with approximate distances for the other irons. Initially, I would suggest writing these down. As you play and practice (and make minor adjustments along the way) the use of certain clubs for certain distances will become second nature. As you improve over time, these numbers might change, just recalibrate.

Everyone will arrive at their own, unique, distance conclusion. Your own personal best distance for a specific club isn't that crucial. It doesn't help our cause to hit the irons as hard as you can every time. You're doing yourself no favors when your #7 iron travels a different distance every time you swing it. The emphasis is on your ability to make similar swings regardless of the club and receive the distance that you are expecting from that swing.

CLUBS USED FOR THE SHORT GAME

Wedges: You will make full swings with these golf clubs, but more than half the time (see chapter 15 Practice) you'll use them with a less than full swing for short game shots. When a full swing will send the ball too far, no matter which golf club you choose, the shot requires a less than full swing. These less than full swings around the greens are enveloped in the phrase 'short game'.

Chipping, Pitching, Sand Shots, and Putting: These are the four facets to the short game. What's the difference between a Chip and a Pitch? I'm glad you asked. It could be some beer and tortillas. No? Sorry, I digress.

In another book you might learn more about technique or mechanics for these shots. Believe me, there is information overload available on the bookshelf. Accept good information from a credible source and do your best to keep it simple (see the chapter 10: Playing the Game). My current objective, however, is to help you feel comfortable on the course, to increase your enjoyment of the game and protect your ego.

It would be better to miss hit the shot than to stare at your golf bag because you have no idea what club to choose. I want you to know each club's job description, but not necessarily discuss the technique of how to use them. Maybe, I'll write that book later.

Here we go. A Chip is a shot in which the ball spends more time rolling than flying. A Pitch is a shot in which the ball spends more time flying than rolling.

For the most part, distance is irrelevant. In fact, a Chip can be a longer shot than a Pitch. Of course, you won't be quizzed on this, but you need to know it if you hear it, and if you say something, you would like it to be correct.

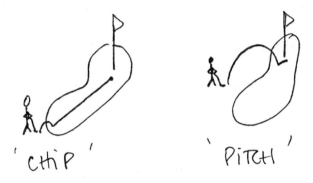

'CHiP'   'PiTCH'

Wedges have really come into golf vogue over the last twenty years or so, and they have been a really hot topic for the last several years. As we dive into this, if you get overwhelmed, take a break, get some oxygen or some gingko and come on back.

There are three basic identifications for the wedges. They are all wedges, but each is specific a type and has a different job. I have already described two variables known as length and lie. For the wedges, length of shaft should not vary too much. The primary difference is in the loft. A secondary difference is a thing that we call 'bounce.'

In a real sense, the Wedges are a continuation of the irons with some adjustments to the clubhead that makes them more conducive to short game shots. Specifically, these adjustments are a more round shape to the sole or flange (bottom), and more weight on the lower portion of the club. Some vendors have even continued the numbering system to include the wedges in the set. They just keep right on going from the #9 iron to a #10 and a #11. This didn't stick. So, we continue to use the lettering system of PW, SW, and LW. These stand for Pitching Wedge, Sand Wedge and Lob Wedge respectively.

Pitching Wedge: The wedge with the least amount of loft (typically 48°-50°) also has the head most like the numbered irons. It is still very manageable with full swings, but has enough loft and weight to be used often around the greens. Some vendors will simply use the letter 'W' to identify the Wedge, because the single term Wedge is synonymous with Pitching Wedge. When the single name Wedge is used, it is usually not referring to a Sand Wedge or Lob Wedge.

Sand Wedge: For a long time this was the most lofted club in the the majority of golf bags (typically 54°-58°). It still has the most weight at the bottom of the clubhead. This weight is shaped specifically to help the clubhead get through the sand and back out again. This is known as 'Bounce.' Without this shape a golf club will tend to dig into the sand rather than rebound out of it. One of golf's great players created bounce by adding weight onto an existing club after visualizing the wing of an airplane. Now, every Sand Wedge that you buy is created that way.

Lob Wedge: Recently, a very lofted category of Wedge has grown in popularity. In fact, many players are now carrying three Wedges, rather than the traditional two. Appropriately named, the objective of the Lob Wedge is to hit the ball very high and not have it roll far after it has landed (typically 60° +/-).

Of course its not possible, but I have set up to hit a shot with a Lob Wedge and wondered if it was going to come up and smack me in the face. There is so much loft on these things, they can get a little squirrely. Be careful making full-swings with the LW. A little like driving in the rain, sometimes they can just get away from you. These Lob Wedges can be used from the sand as well and like the SW are available with a variety of loft/bounce options.

As the loft is measured in degrees, the bounce is measure in degrees, and you will see the family of wedges marketed and sold with these dimensions. Golf Club manufacturers cover virtually any combination that you and your local PGA Professional determine is best for your game.

Putter: The objective is self-evident. You want to roll the ball into the hole. There are many vendors using any number of marketing techniques to sell putters. Admittedly, some of the hi-tech stuff is valid, but when push comes to shove we're all using a shaft with a flat face at the bottom. Go practice.

PROPERLY EQUIPPED

You don't want to go out and buy 14 different golf clubs from 14 different vendors; a golf bag smorgasborg. The set needs to have a certain amount of continuity. Also, you want them to be appealing.

Your golf clubs are something that you will become comfortable with, something that you can rely on. So, don't be afraid to get them dirty. If they're new, you might even bang them around a little before you go play. As an added bonus, this might help you look like a veteran.

For the numbered irons, make sure that you buy a set and that set is one model from one vendor. Until you really know your way around, it's probably best to stay with this same vendor for your wedges as well. Down the line, you can mix and match your wedges as you see fit.

I have already discussed the length, shaft flex, and loft of the golf clubs. You now know that each golf club will be slightly different in make-up in order to produce a different result. If you assemble a 'set' of clubs from a variety of vendors, you might end up with 2 or 3 golf clubs that will produce the same result. This is defeating the purpose.

The woods are in a different category. They do not need to be from the same vendor as your numbered irons or wedges. However, for the time being, only use one specific vendor for all your woods. Later, you may choose to have a driver from one vendor and a fairway wood from another.

To recap, with the woods, you should choose one vendor. This same or another single vendor should be chosen for the numbered irons and the wedges. The putter is completely personal preference. It doesn't have to match anything and can come from any type from any vendor that you like.

Although no two sets of golf clubs are alike, here are some models. For a 'starter' or partial set this is a good selection;

• #3, #5 wood; #4, #6, #8, PW, SW; Putter

When you have all fourteen, here are a few ways it can look;

• Driver; #3, #5, #7 wood; #3, #4, #5, #6, #7, #8, #9, PW, SW; Putter

• Driver; #3, #5, wood; #3, #4, #5, #6, #7, #8, #9, PW, SW, LW; Putter

• #3, #5, #7 wood; #3, #4, #5, #6, #7, #8, #9, PW, SW, LW; Putter

From Driver to Lob Wedge your golf clubs have a purpose. Get some golf clubs that fit you and are appealing to the eye. Once you have them, take some quality practice time to get some research done. A wise man once said, 'Luck...is preparation meeting opportunity'. This has never been more true than in the game of golf. Candidly, even Tour players make bad choices on the golf course. But what they don't do is make excuses after the fact. Prepare yourself to make your best decision on the golf course. Make your best swing and pose like you know what you're doing.

Next, regardless of result, return the club to the bag and walk down the fairway. With a confident swagger, smell the roses, soak in the landscape and thank God for a great day.

Chapter 8

WEATHER

It was my distinct pleasure to work with Mr. Bill Ninnis. Bill had retired from his 'real' job as a General Contractor and was now enjoying his occupation in the golf business, working in the Pro Shop. His university degree in psychology came in handy during some discussions about human behavior, as it seemed that some players (God bless them) were simply golf addicts. It was an inability to say 'no'. Late to appointments, skipped appointments, broken marriages, darkness, was there a limit? There was one day that will always stand out in my mind.

In the late 1990's we began a year in which the Bay Area received rain on each of the first twenty-one days of January. Many golf courses were closed and the courses that were 'open' were not really playable. From what I recall, it was on day 'eighteen' of this stretch that I got a phone call.

"Hey, how's the weather there?" the voice on the line inquired. Before the internal chuckle became an external laugh, I stopped myself.'This guy must be calling from out-of-town," I thought. He could have been from Tempe or Albuquerque, or the face of the Sun. Let's give him the benefit of the doubt. Gently I asked, "Sir, where are you calling from?" Without hesitation he replied, "Oh, I'm a couple of miles away."

The game that we love is played within nature. Truth be told, that is one of the reasons we like it. More than a simple meeting with clients, a social event, or competition with the buddies, it is the breath of fresh air or a conquering of the elements.

Nature is not always cooperative, however. Rain, sleet, snow, and even things beyond the postal service motto, like fog and frost, can be a challenge for humans and golf balls alike. Although some of these forces prohibit even the most addicted, other conditions should be braved by anyone of reasonable mind and body. There is a name for those who refuse to participate in anything less than an ideal forecast, with an appropriate lack of respect, we call them 'fair weather golfers'. For the rest of us, here are some do's and don'ts for less than perfect conditions.

Forecasting -

"When's it going to rain?" Perhaps, this is a simple question, but consider the answer. When bad weather is near the Golf Shop Staff makes a remarkable transformation. The new addition to the job description is 'expert meteorologist.' Now, you might think that it would be a flattering misnomer, but here's the problem; they don't know when it will rain either. After being pressed on the issue for a while, it just seems best to start offering guesses. *"How's about 11:30am?"* On a more humorous note, I knew of an 'expert' who would inform the caller that it was 80° and sunny, no matter what the conditions. You could count on the reply, "Really?"

Rain – Your Weather Guesser might be able to tell you the difference between Rain and Showers. As for me it doesn't really matter until you can't keep anything dry. A mist is no problem, a sprinkle can be fun, rain is workable for a while, but when you can't hold the club, that's when it's too much.

The best advice for rain is this; buy the best Rain Gear that you can afford. Make absolutely certain that it fits you. Don't buy a 'rain suit' that only gives you a matching jacket (top) and the pants (bottom). One usually fits, the other doesn't. Go with a Vendor that will produce a jacket that fits and pants that fit. Buy them both, once time. Unless you are a Junior, this purchase should last you for the rest of your life. (MSRP $250+/-)

A waterproof hat is a good idea. Most of these caps will remind you of your dad's fishing hat, but forget the fashion faux pas, you are simply trying to stay dry. (MSRP $30 +/-)

Gloves that are designed for wet conditions are now available. Remarkably, one manufacturer recommends that you soak the gloves (sold in pairs) before use on the course. These aren't for everybody, but if they feel comfortable, it might be an advantage on a cold, wet day. (MSRP $25 +/-)

Frost – Loosely defined, when the temperature is near freezing (32°f) and the dew point creates moisture, Frost can form. This is different from the ground freezing. When Frost forms the blade of grass is frozen, but the ground is not. Thus the problem. With pressure on the grass (by walking or driving a cart) the blade might break at the base and it will die.

When the possibility of Frost exists (clear sky and cool temperatures), the Golf Course Superintendent must test the areas of the course that are prone to Frost. Should the Frost be present, we need to make sure that play does not begin until the Frost is gone. This is known as a Frost Delay. There is no exact measurement of how long it will take for this Delay to be 'lifted', but the experienced Superintendent will have a good guess. Go get some breakfast, buy something in the Golf Shop, or read the newspaper.

There are a couple of different ways to manage the affect the delay will have on the day's play. Neither is a perfect solution and there are positives and negatives to both. One way is to simply bump back the starting times relative to the amount of delay. The Starting Time of 7:30am would become 9:00am with an hour and a half Frost Delay. There is a certain amount of inconvenience for those who are delayed early on (maybe Aunt Martha's wedding is at 2:00pm), but the real bummer is the group that was supposed to start at 1:00pm. With the domino effect (or trickle down) this has been pushed back to a 2:30pm reservation and they will not complete their round due to darkness.

The other way to administrate this is to start the day at the point on the Tee Sheet where the Frost Delay lifted. When the delay is lifted at 9:00am that becomes the first group sent out for the day. They and everyone else after them is on time. This will essentially erase all reservations prior to allowing play.

For 75% of the golfers this is a great solution. Some would even say, "Hey, its the cool and clear season, that's what they get for making an early reservation." With reservations sometimes being available thirty days in advance that is pretty cold (pardon the pun). The other 25% isn't totally out of luck. The Golf Shop can seize any opportunity, like a 'no show', to get these groups on the course as soon as possible.

Darned if you do and darned if you don't. Should the policy annoy everyone and push back the entire day? Misery does love company. Or, should the procedure annoy just 25% while making the vast majority happy? This is the debate.

Unless you live in Hawaii or Florida, ask your Pro Shop what there policy is. Schedule your starting time accordingly. If its cold and clear, give them a call the morning that you are scheduled to play and ask them if they had a Delay.

Fog - Similar, but not as potentially damaging to the course is Fog. Sometimes you just can't see. Usually, there is no delay in the event of Fog. Hopefully, a forecaddie or spotter will assist with the locating of golf balls. If there is not, then go ahead and hit when the Starter gives you permission and do your best.

Darkness - With an exemption for those on vacation, it gets dark at the Golf Course at the same time the sun goes down at your house. Maybe its fifteen years of phone calls talking, but it is amazing how many local people (ironically tourists don't ask this one) call and ask, "What time does it get dark?"

Hot - There really aren't any 'Veteran' moves to relate to you here. Go with what makes you comfortable and use common sense. When temperatures get in the triple digits drink a lot of water, wear a hat, and bring more than one glove. As your hand perspires, switch to the dry glove.

Sunscreen - If you decide to wear sunscreen, choose a sunscreen that will not make your hand greasy. More and more Vendors are creating sunscreens designed with sports in mind. You can even purchase a 'spray-on,' rather than using a cream or lotion, this way it will not get on your hands. Your local Pro Shop should have a good selection.

Top Dressed Greens - Also known to the players as 'aerification' (although you won't find it in Webster's) this seasonal procedure will affect golfers in the spring and fall. The golf course maintenance crew will punch holes in the greens and then back-fill them with sand. Even though the excess sand is removed and the green is groomed to be as smooth as possible, the putting surface will not return to normal for 2 - 3 weeks.

This needs to be done a couple of times a year for the average golf course. It opens up the root base, helps retard thatch (organic growth), and is a component to good drainage.

If this doesn't bother you, that's great. If so, right around March - April in the spring and September - October in the fall, phone the Pro Shop and check to see when this process is scheduled.

When you're playing in inclement conditions, just keep plugging away and have fun. The truth of the matter is that many of the people or competitors that you play with will mentally give in to the weather. So, if you can keep your wits about you and play your game, success is well within your grasp.

Chapter 9

A BRIEF HISTORY

Four friends on holiday in Scotland had already finished a morning round of golf. The afternoon was spent at several local pubs, stopping at each for a pint (known as a 'pub-crawl'). Later, they came to a barely lucid decision to get in another round at golf's oldest course.

At the Old Course in St. Andrews, the oldest golf course in the world, the first hole and the eighteenth hole are parallel to each other. The beginning of the course and the end of the course are within a stones throw. They share the same piece of turf. This places the first tee and the eighteenth green side by side.

Greens fees were paid and caddies assigned. Barely able to put the ball on the tee, the first participant then troubled himself to take a swipe at the ball. The next player took a mighty cut and the ball dribbled across the grass, but in the direction of the fairway. After the third player fared no better, the final player took the Tee. A lefty, he bent over, coaxed the ball on the tee, and addressed the ball. The dysfunctional motion caused the ball to be struck directly off the end of the clubhead and flew across the first tee and onto the eighteenth green near the flagstick. In that inimitable Scottish droll, his caddy bellowed, "Great shot, sir. If ya make the putt, you'll go 'round in two!"

No one really knows where golf began; as a result some would say that the spirit of the game is not bound by time. At some points in history, golf was a game of the wealthy, but now in these United States, virtually anyone who has the desire is able to play. We should be grateful, for this is a more recent privilege. Around the globe, the game is played by millions of people in hundreds of countries.

Who first played the game with a stick and a ball? Was it Roman soldiers? Chinese in the Ming Dynasty? Dutch playing a game on ice? English paintings depict the game. Belgium had a similar team game. Or, was its beginning a form of Croquet that the French played in Normandy? The exact origin is unknown, but what we do know is that the Scots gave golf its definition.

The first official document regarding the game was an edict by James II in 1457, banning golf due to the amount of time spent playing the game rather than working. James the IV complained because the military men were choosing to play golf over honing their military skills. It is said that in 1567, Mary, Queen of Scots, played Golf the day after her husband was murdered.

The game was being played for over 400 years before there was a Golf Course or any written rules. So, you have Joe and Ernie, or rather Robert the Bruce and William Wallace, with a stick and a ball. They pick a starting point and a finishing point and whoever completes this in the least amount of strokes is the winner. Think about it, this would have been fun.

EARLY COMPETITIONS

My first experience at a private club was as an Assistant Professional in Oakland, CA. We used to play a variation of the game that we called 'cross country'. From the 6th tee, we would play to the 18th green. From the 5th tee to the 8th green. Just pick a starting point and a finishing hole. Those were the days.

Of course this would make it difficult to host a competition. You need some parameters, an answer to all of the 'could of', 'would of', and 'what about' questions. The first organized competition took place in 1744 with the Gentleman Golfers of Leith. This necessitated the first written Rules of Golf of which there were thirteen (see Chapter 18: Rules).

Since there were no rules the 'golf courses' had little to no parameters, either. You can imagine that the courses bore little resemblance to the manicured fairways that we know today. Large areas were maintained by default through Oceanside conditions and grazing animals. The feeding of sheep and goats can keep grass relatively short and remarkably consistent. When the bad weather would come, the sheep would burrow themselves into large holes (or bunker), and later the wind would bring in a layer of sand. A rabbit possibly created the finishing point or 'hole' and the 'tee' was a scoop full of sand placed within inches of the previous hole.

THE ORIGINAL COURSE

The original course at St. Andrews at one point had a total of 22 'holes'. Players would play 11 holes going away, or 'out'. Then turn around and return by playing them 'in'. We still use these terms today. Two of these holes were removed and the course was reduced to a total of 18, nine 'out' and nine 'in'. This number held and became the basis for all golf courses.

THE FIRST GOLF CLUB

In 1754, the first Golf Club (group of golfers) was formed. As the number of clubs grew, the need for a government arose to bring consistency to the Rules and Organizations. With seventeen known Golf Clubs; fourteen in Scotland, two in England, and one in India (created by an Englishman), the Royal and Ancient Golf Club of St. Andrews, Scotland, was established in 1834.

The popularity of golf was growing, but the costs kept the game from being played by everyone. Ironically, it wasn't the Greens Fees or the exorbitant Club Membership, since any large, flat space would suffice. It was the equipment.

EARLY EQUIPMENT

The clubs weren't cheap and the balls were really expensive. The ball of this day had a leather cover, was filled with feathers and was called the 'feathery'. Three strips of leather were sewn together leaving a small slit. A Top Hat full of feathers was then soaked in water. The wet feathers were stuffed through the slit into the ball. When the feathers dried and the leather hardened the ball was ready to go. Unfortunately, one person could only produce about 3 or 4 of these Feathery balls per day. Players would lose 3 to 4 balls per round. If you do the math, it would cost more than a day's wages to play a round of golf.

A 19th Century English man happened upon some material from a Malayan Gum Tree. This material was like rubber and when heated could be rolled into balls. When the rubber cooled, it would harden and be ready for play. This changed golf. Not only for the consistency of those who already played, but also one could produce 100 per day and the material was not expensive. This 'gutta percha' ball made golf far more affordable. More people were playing the game.

THE GROWTH OF GOLF

Another component to Golf's expansion was the railroad. Golf Clubs in Edinburgh, Leith and Prestwick were joined by rail to St. Andrews and in 1860, the first 'Professional' tournament was held. The inaugural champion won a Silver Club, which was akin to the Archery trophy of the day. The following year, it became an 'open' tournament with amateurs being included and the victor would earn a Champions Belt. The winner's spoil would change again to a trophy known as the Claret Jug. To this day, it is awarded to the winner of what is now known as the British Open Championship. Granted, here in the States we make the distinction of 'British'. To those in Great Britain, it remains simply the 'Open Championship.'

By 1890 there were 387 clubs and 140 different golf courses. With the new balls, the players called for development in the type of clubs. The lighter, more consistent balls could be struck with lighter, more flexible shafts. Golf Clubs made the move from Hazel and Ash to Hickory and Beachwood.

GOLF IN THE UNITED STATES

After a purchase at St. Andrews, a man named Lockhart brought six golf clubs across the pond to the States. The year was 1888. Things must have caught on quickly, because in the fall of the same year our first Golf Club was established. Also called St. Andrews Golf Club, this was the beginning of organized golf in the United States.

TOURNAMENT GOLF

Our first national tournament, the U.S. Amateur was held in 1894. That same year five of the leading Golf Clubs came together to create what would become the United States Golf Association. Like the Royal and Ancient overseas, this body continues to lead in the United States.

Equipment made another advance near 1900 with a ball that was similar in concept to a baseball. With a rubber core surrounded by windings and then a cover, this ball would become the ball of choice for the next hundred years. Around this time the golf clubs changed as well, with the type of wood changing to Persimmon and shafts making the transition from Hickory to steel.

Yet perhaps the most influential event in the early 1900's was the first United States golf hero. Francis Ouimet decided to enter the 1913 US Open to be close to the great players. Winning was not probable. Some might say impossible. However, after a playoff with the era's greats Varden and Ray, Ouimet outplayed them both and gave the golf world something and someone to believe in.

PLAYING GOLF FOR A LIVING

The golfing population swelled from 350,000 to 2,000,000. Although at that time no one thought of making a living playing golf. Golf Professionals had home clubs where they re-gripped clubs and gave golf lessons.

It wasn't until the Twentieth Century that a group of Gentleman got together and developed a series of events for those who would play the game for a living and in 1916, the Professional Golfer's Association of America was born.

Playing Tournament Golf with money as the prize began just a little more than a hundred years ago. Playing Golf with the intention of making it a career has evolved over the last seventy to eighty years. The 'tour' was barely that, with a few events in the summer or for those in the South a couple of dates in the winter.

TAKING THE SHOW ON THE ROAD

Gentlemen would travel from property to property and either entertain through exhibitions or compete in Tournaments for Professionals. Primarily, these locations were arranged in a geographical order enabling the participants to make short sequential trips. On a map it might look like the cross-county run of a Greyhound bus, or simply, the Tour.

With modern transportation today's Tours might look more like a phone operator's switchboard, but some of the geographical concerns still hold true. It's just that now these concerns have more to do with weather than with the players' ability to get from one location to the next.

Currently, there are a number of 'Tours.' The PGA Tour, The LPGA Tour (ladies), and the Champions Tour (seniors) to name a few.

On balance, a Tour starts off in the West. Somewhere near the end of January they will make their way through Arizona. Then on to the San Francisco Bay Area, Los Angeles, Palm Springs and maybe another Arizona spot. In March or early April, it's off to Florida where the Tour will stay in the South for several weeks. Right around June, the Mid-West will be host until the end of July, when it's appropriate to head east and visit New England.

THE MAJORS

Even though all of the events are important and every player's performance will dictate their future on the tour, there are a half a dozen key tournaments including four so-called Majors. A victory in one of these Championships can solidify a successful career on the Tour.

For the women, they are known as the Dinah Shore, the LPGA Championship, the ladies' U.S. Open, and the ladies' British Open. For the men they are the Masters' Tournament, the U.S. Open, the British Open, and the PGA Championship. There is one more to mention for the men, the Players' Championship held each spring in Florida.

THE PRINCIPALS

All born in 1912, three men became Golf's Champions for the forties and fifties and in large part were responsible for growth of the game. In the year, 1945, Byron Nelson had the best year of any Golf Professional before or after. Out of a possible 35 events he won 18 times and during one stretch, he won 11 in a row. He had a scoring average of 68.33, never finished worse than 9th, and won $63,000. Put in today's terms, he would have over $10,000,000.

Sam Snead, possessing golf's most fluid swing, won 84 Tournaments over his career, more than anyone else. In fact, he is the oldest player to win a PGA Tour event and won in an event in every year from the 1947 to 1962.

Heroically, Ben Hogan played his most renowned golf after being told he would never play again. In 1946, out of possible 32 tournaments, Hogan won 13 times. However, driving from one Tour event to another, a bus hit Mr. Hogan's car and his legs were severely damaged. He would not make a full physical recovery. For each round he played, his legs would be tightly wrapped and following play his legs would be treated. But, he would be able to walk and continue to swing the golf club with unmatched precision.

After the accident he perhaps played his best golf. On a restricted schedule, he won almost every time he played. One year, 1953, in limited action due to his injuries, he won the Masters, the US Open and the British Open (in his only appearance).

The men weren't the only ones having fun. Babe Zaharias was one of the best female athletes of her time. She won medals in the 1932 Olympics and took up golf to win a host of events including the 1950 LPGA Championship.

Patty Berg, a former US Marine (remember this is the 1940's), took up golf and had 44 wins.

TELEVISION

With the advent of television, came golf's most influential player. The timing was impeccable. Arnold Palmer was not the typical Country Club player. He had a 'no holds barred' attitude, a rugged appearance, and an awesome golf game.

His style of play and the way that he carried himself made the game attractive to millions of viewers.

Palmer won over 60 PGA events, was the first Tour Player to hire an agent and the first to earn $100,000 in a single year. His fans were so loyal, they were called 'Arnie's Army'.

From 1960 to 1970 the US golfing population doubled from 5 million to over 10 million and the number of golf courses grew from 6,300 to over 10,000. Essentially, a golf course opened everyday for ten straight years.

GOLF COURSE ARCHITECTS

During this same stretch, golf course design became a profession. Before this time, designing golf courses was not a primary source of income. With the increasing popularity and the number of golf courses being built, it was possible for those with the talent and desire to leave their day job. Beginning in 1945, Robert Trent Jones took part in designing over 500 golf courses and lifted the building of a golf course to the level of Architecture.

There have been many golf course Architects, but only some are well known for their work. Ress Jones (son of Robert Trent Jones), Robert Trent Jones, Jr., Pete Dye, Alister Mackenzie, Tom Weiskoff, Pete Fazio, Arnold Palmer, Jack Nicklaus to name a few. But the most curious is Jack Neville. If you like to go out on top, I suppose this is what you do. The only golf course Neville ever designed was the Pebble Beach Golf Links.

GOLF TODAY

Today, over 35,000,000 people participate in the game of golf at nearly 16,000 golf courses across the United States. Many properties and players have become household names. The game has come a long way and there is a bright future. What once was a game for the elite, or the rich, has become an adventure that is available to anyone who has the desire to play. No one really knows how golf began, but the spirit of the game is timeless.

Chapter 10

PLAYING THE GAME

My father-in-law, Bob Whitehead, really looked forward to a round of Golf on a quality Course. For that matter he was very passionate about virtually everything that he did. Due to his schedule, he only played about half-a-dozen rounds a year and most of those took place on our family vacations.

His enjoyment of the game was not a result of his scores, but sometimes he would decide that he was going to take a round or a shot seriously. On just such an occasion he took into account every conceivable variable prior to making his next swing. Distance, wind, humidity, barometric pressure, and the earth's rotation, were all calibrated and reconciled. Upon completion of his golf swing, the ball came to rest about ten feet nearer the target than it started. After advancing to this new location, he turned to me and stated with conviction, "I guess it's the same from here."

Many books, videos, seminars, and lessons on 'game improvement' are available. Keep in mind; the purpose of the book that you are reading is not necessarily to lower your scores. Becoming a better player may or may not increase your love for the Game. The objective is to make you more comfortable on the Golf Course, to impress your clients or friends, and to increase your *enjoyment* of the Game.

However, continuing to improve your skills and making progress in the game can be a component to its enjoyment. Over the last fifteen years, I have had the opportunity to work with many players. From the junior who has never touched a club, to the player preparing for the Tour, it as been my pleasure to teach and to work for players of all ages and skill levels. My teaching philosophy is simple. There are basic principles and fundamental motions that will enable all of us to become good players. At the same time, no two people are alike. We are all different. In my opinion, it is important to teach foundational, common denominators and allow each player's own personality, style and rhythm to come through in building a repetitive swing.

The motions of Sport have common threads; hitting a Tennis Ball solid, kicking a Football consistently through the uprights, throwing Strikes, rolling a Bowling Ball over the right board, in order to do these things effectively a player must have good mechanics. It was no wonder to me that the best golfers from the other Major Sports are football kickers and baseball pitchers.

When it comes to developing a repetitive golf swing, keep it simple. As one of football's greatest coaches said to his struggling team, "Gentlemen, this is a football."

It is our desire for the golf ball to fly toward the target. In order for the golf ball to fly toward the target, the golf club must move toward the target. As such, for the golf club to move toward the target, your body must move toward the target. Sounds simple, huh? Well in a way it is, but we are human and no one is perfect. However, as you absorb good information and train your body to make good motions, you can become a more consistent player.

With the assumption that you have already received a certain amount of instruction, begin by making sure that your address position is sound. Properly align toward your target, grip the golf club correctly, and put your body in an athletic posture. Now you are in a position to make a good swing.

Even though you have already 'learned' these, do not take them for granted. Continue to practice a good address position.

With regard to the swing itself, the base of your golf swing is the motion that your body makes. When I teach my students, I like to talk about the swing using the analogy of a house. All of us have our own body, our own swing, and our own house. There are designs for structures that stand up over time and the plan for your house (golf swing) calls for a solid foundation of good balance and good body positions.

The cornerstone of this foundation is the move that your body makes toward the target. It is that integral part upon which everything else depends. If our goal in the game is to hit the ball in the direction of the target, it only makes sense that our body must move in that direction as well. Granted, it is not the only part of a swing, but without an effective forward motion we are sunk.

You would like to put your body into the correct positions in order for your arms and hands and golf club to be free to assume correct positions. This is why it is called a 'swing' and not a 'hit'.

So, until further notice, try not to get too caught up with your back-swing. Later, you will learn more about the back-swing, but until you are able to move forward effectively, your back-swing is a secondary issue. Think about it. If you have a perfect backswing, but cannot move forward, how well will you strike the ball? We don't even need to have an orthodox back-swing to have a productive swing. A solid forward motion can cover a multitude of sins.

How do you know if you are on your way to good, repeatable body motions? The evidence is in your ability to finish your swing in a position that faces the target and is steady. Every time you swing, try to finish with your belt buckle facing the target and your spine is fairly vertical. Stay there for a few moments to verify that you are balanced and in a secure position. This is a good foundation. Of course, not every shot will be perfect, but you will hit a greater number of good shots. If worse comes to worse, this pose will help you look like you know what you're doing.

That having been said, Golf Lessons are a must. How many of you would try to teach yourself martial arts? Intriguingly, there are many similarities including; balance, body position, leverage and a mental side to the activity. Yet, we do hear 'resistance' to lessons; "I just started and I'm going to play for a while before I take lessons," or "I'm not sure what those guys could teach me that I don't already know."

Regarding the first objection, your local PGA/LPGA instructor will save you many hours of frustration and lost golf balls. When I first started playing, I heard that Lee Trevino (one of golf's greats) had never taken a golf lesson. This was my inspiration to never spend a dime, or put my ego on the line by exposing any flaws to an instructor. My ego and wallet took a different form of punishment (through poor play in competition) until I was willing to ask some questions.

Next, remember that Tiger Woods, and every other Tour player for that matter has an Instructor. Even if you think that you have a good understanding of the swing, you can't see yourself. *(See chapter 14: Lessons)*

There are just a few more things that I want to share with you about hitting shots on the course. These are things that will improve your enjoyment of the game and of course, make you look like a veteran.

Establish a pre-swing routine. This is a deliberate set of thoughts and motions that you will initiate prior to every golf swing. When you develop a familiar set of movements before you make your swing, it will increase your confidence in the swing itself.

You have your own personality and style that will be a part of the make-up, but here are some suggestions on how to form this routine. Start behind the ball and identify your target line. Take a practice swing, a 'dress rehearsal'. Next, move up alongside your golf ball and assume a correct address position. When your body is situated, look toward the target and make sure that everything is in order. As soon as you are comfortable, begin your swing.

It doesn't matter how, it's how many. Practically, you just want to get the ball in the hole in as few strokes as possible. Philosophically, you should use whatever golf club, or type of shot it takes to get the job done. Many people get caught up in the notion that certain things have to be done a certain way. Fundamentals are the foundation for a repetitive golf swing. At the same time, those fundamentals allow for your individuality. There are many different types of 'houses' built on solid foundations.

A few years ago, I was blessed to accompany a group from our local Club to participate in an event in Pinehurst, North Carolina. Pinehurst #2 had just been host to the US Open golf championship. The putting greens are set up like upside-down bowls or as a television analyst said it was like grass on top of a Volkswagen Beetle.

The problem was that after the ball hit the green, it would invariably roll off the other side of the bowl. Only a well struck shot would hit and hold. The area around the greens was a challenge also. A chip or pitch that would fly to the green would often roll past the flagstick, or even across the green and down the other side.

Hanging around the Clubhouse, hitting a few short game shots, I see this guy essentially bunting balls through the fringe and up onto the green. He was using a 3-wood and a 7-iron with 20' to the hole, essentially rolling the ball through the longer grass and up onto the Putting Green and next to the pin. This wasn't necessarily new, but the type of courses that I was familiar with didn't require that shot, or at least the need wasn't great enough for me to practice that shot. A couple of hours later, that shot worked for me, too.

Getting the ball in the hole is the point. One of golf's greats once said, "If you can shank it the same every time, shank it." There are many orthodox motions and shots that should be used on a regular basis, but don't be afraid to try something new or different.

Also, as one of our favorite action film stars has said, "...a man's got to know his limitations". Hit the shot that you feel comfortable with, the shot that will put you in a better position.

Hit the shot that puts the ball closer to the hole, or makes your next shot easier. If you are off the green and think that using the Putter is the odds on way to get the ball near the hole, do it. If you are uncomfortable in the sand, use the club that you need to get the ball out. It might be a putter for that shot, too.

Finally, on this topic of playing the game, I am often asked about the best Instructional Book on Golf. Realistically, there can be no single book that covers it all, says everything, or states it economically. Let me recommend several from my bookshelf; Hogan's Five Modern Fundamentals, by Ben Hogan; The Perfect Swing, by Jimmy Ballard; Short Game Book, by Dave Pelz; The Golf Swing, by David Leadbetter; and The Master Key by Leslie King.

These books contain some very good information and will be a component in your education. They will help put you in a position to develop a solid swing and an adept short game. However, you can't see yourself and each of you has a different body and a unique style that is a part of who you are. Your local PGA or LPGA Professional needs to be a part of your game improvement program.

Now, you get to take it to the course. Of course, a round of golf is not the place to work on things or a place to let your mind get caught up with mechanical issues. Keep it basic, focus on a couple of topics, and have fun. In fact, your ability to keep it simple will allow you to stay calm about the game and enjoy the day with your group.

Chapter 11

TYPES OF PLAY

There is an exclusive, private club in Pebble Beach, California, is one of handful of golf courses that I would give a lot to play just once in my life. The golf course is positioned on the Monterey Bay and a few of the holes have breathtaking views of the ocean and coastline. Divine providence has allowed me to play there more than once.

The Club has received different opinions on how they operate the golf course, but this does not deter the Membership from doing what they think is best.

During my most recent round, as we made our way across the 17th tee, I asked one person in the group about a buoy that was several hundred yards off shore. He said, "Oh, that's our suggestion box."

In one sense there is only one way to play the game: to get the ball in the hole with as few strokes as possible. From another view, the game can be played in a variety of styles and formats. There are even different ways to keep score.

The two basic types of competition are Stroke Play and Match Play;

In **Stroke Play,** You simply count the number of strokes (and penalty strokes) in order to arrive at a total. The player who completes the round in the fewest number of strokes is the winner. This is the predominant format on Television. The Tour players complete multiple rounds with the winner having the lowest aggregate total.

In **Match Play,** the game is played on a hole by hole basis. A hole is 'won' by the player or team who completes the hole in the fewest number of strokes. After a hole is completed, the number of strokes tallied will not come up again.

That hole is over and it is either a win or a loss. For example, if Joe has 8 strokes on the hole and Jane has 4 strokes on the hole, Jane wins the hole. The fact that she won by 4 strokes is now moot, because Jane has won the hole. The player or team that is leading by a number of holes greater than the number of holes remaining wins the Match. Virtually all on-course wagers use this type of play. *(See Chapter 13: Place your Bets)*

Using these two basic types of play, the world of golf has come up with several different ways to host an entertaining competition.

Types of Scoring in Stroke Play --

First, we have traditional Stroke Play. Just keep track of the number of times you made an attempt to hit the ball and penalty strokes. That is your total. This can be used for a single round or events with multiple rounds.

Next we have Stableford. The player's score is converted using a reward system in which par is neutral. Here's how the system works:

Double Eagle: 8 points	**Birdie:** 2 points	**Bogey:** -1 point
Eagle: 5 points	**Par:** 0 points	**Double Bogey or Worse:** -3 pts

After each hole is completed and the strokes are translated, you add up the point totals. A player who made 'birdie' and then 'eagle' would have a total of 7 points. If a 'bogey' is then converted and added to the score, the player would then have a total of 6 points. Par on every hole would result in a final total of zero. Seems a bit understated for a round of even par, doesn't it?

There are several varieties of this format and the one just described is known 'Modified Stableford'. There is a tour using this version in an event called the 'International' that is played in Colorado. Other versions simply adjust the number of points awarded by category. For example, a converted 'birdie' would only give you 1 point and a 'double bogey' might only cost you -2 points.

Match Play –

Again, in this format, it is a hole by hole event, with holes simply won or lost. With Match Play there is no sense in changing the way that you keep score, because it will always end up either a won or lost hole.

Let's go into the terminology a little deeper. The player or team (side) who has the least number of strokes on a given hole has 'won' that hole. If the players tie the hole, the hole is 'halved.' The winner is the side that is leading by a number of holes greater than the number of holes remaining. A player or team is 'dormie' when they are ahead by as many holes remain to be played (i.e. 3 holes UP with 3 holes to play). *(Rules of Golf, Rule 2)*

With this type of play and because your opponent(s) is in the same group, some of the Rules are different. I won't go into all of them, but there is one that you will need to know right away. A player or team may concede a hole or match at any time prior to the conclusion of the hole or match. This is important and it will come into play in the Chapter on Betting *(Chapter 15)*.

Conceding a shot or hole or match -

On your first shot, for example, you 'knock it (the ball) stiff' and have an easy putt for birdie. Your opponent is hitting his third ball off the tee. The first shot made a splashing sound in the water on one side and the second flew into a row of houses on the other. To save time and agony, he is able concede that he will lose this hole. Rather than keep playing and hope against hope, he is able to send up the white flag and surrender. Why waste precious energy? When he has made his decision, it will sound like this, 'I concede the hole.' Concession of an entire hole is not done very often, so it requires that well enunciated phrase.

On the Putting Green this is done a little differently. Eventually, a ball will come to rest at point blank range. Also, the ball does not have to go into the hole to determine the winner and at this point the winner might be all but determined. Sometimes it is done out of respect or for speed of play. When you or your opponent decide to concede that stroke (and in turn the hole) you do so by stating that your opponent's next Putt is 'good'. The phrase that you will hear is, 'Its good.'

As you have learned, experienced golfers look for different ways of saying the same thing. So, you might hear; 'take it away,' or 'I don't want to see any more of that.' These are phrases for the convivial match. If you are ever in a Tournament with an Entry Fee, stick with the basic 'That's good' and say it loud and clear.

Team Play--

Four-ball: Very often a group of four players will divide themselves into pairs for the purpose of a Match. Also known as 'best-ball' or 'better ball', the most common form of team competition today is technically called Four-ball. This is a Match in which two play their better ball against the better ball of two other players.

All four play their own ball. Upon completion of the hole, the lower individual score of one pair is compared to the other. The lower score wins the hole. Lets draw this out. Jane and Joe are playing a four-ball match against Steve and Stephi. On the first hole Jane makes 5, Joe makes 6, Steve makes 7 and Stephi makes 8. The better ball of Jane & Joe is 5 and the better ball of Steve & Stephi is 7. Jane and Joe win the first hole. Their position is known as 1 UP.

HOLE NUMBER	1	2	3	4	5	6
YARDAGE	400	208	550	420	380	390
HANDICAP	5	11	13	3	7	9
JANE	5	5				
JOE	6	6				
STEPHi	8	2				
STEVE	7	4				
JANE & JOE	+1	AS				

SCORECARD EXAMPLE

The second hole finds Stephi with a tap-in birdie and a score of 2. Steve made a 4, while Jane made 5 and Joe made 6. Jane & Joe concede Steve's birdie putt and Steve & Stephi win the hole. Jane & Joe are no longer 1 UP. By losing the hole their 1 UP is now neutral and The Match is known as All Square.

This Match could see-saw back and forth or one side could take a commanding lead. As soon as a lead is larger than the remaining holes, that side has won.

Foursome: This is probably the most improperly used word in golf. This is not a generic term for four people playing in the same group. This word describes a form of play in which two players play against two players and each team (side) plays only one ball. In a set rotation, players from each side alternate shots.

Although the proper term is Foursome, this form of play has also been called Alternate Shot or Scotch. In fact, there are variations of play that have been identified as Modified Scotch. These varieties can be fun. In one variety, Modified Scotch, both players hit from the tee. In the fairway they choose one of the balls for the next shot. The other ball is picked up. The players then alternate shots with the one ball until it is holed.

Scramble: the novice player often incorrectly calls this form of play 'best-ball' or 'better-ball'. This becomes golf's second most popular misnomer. As you now know, these words already have other definitions.

Often used in Charity or Company golf events, this format has all four players in the group hitting a Tee shot. The best of the four shots is chosen. The other three are picked up. All four players then hit from the spot of the best shot. This procedure is continued until the ball is in the hole.

There are variations and your Course Handicap can be used with this format as well, primarily with the objective of establishing a fair playing field. My favorite is called the Pinehurst Scramble. In this format, the player whose ball is chosen cannot hit the following shot. Tell that one to you boss or fundraising chairperson.

Fourball, Foursome, and Match Play -- Try these with your friends. Golfers have enjoyed these forms of play for centuries. In fact, the Tour used Match Play until television became a factor. Television has obviously done great things for golf by increasing golf's exposure and enhancing revenue to the respective tours, but one unfortunate result of television is the reduction of Match Play.

With Stroke Play, you can count on an eighteen hole round. Every player must play every hole. A Match, however, could end as early as the 11th Tee. There goes some valuable commercial time. Therefore, Match Play is not very popular with advertisers. As a result, the general golfing population has been limited to their exposure of different forms of play.

Remarkably, as I reminisce on fifteen years of golf business employment, I can't recall one time that I saw or even heard of a group (outside of an organized event) playing a Foursome Match. It would be fun to have a Starter or Marshal scratch their head when they realize that out of the four players walking down the fairway, only two of them hit a tee shot.

Chapter 12

IT'S NOT A DISABILITY,
IT'S A HANDICAP

Imagine that the friends in your golf club are now impressed with your golf prowess. Thanks to your local PGA Professional and this book, you are getting comfortable on the course or maybe even a little cocky. Maybe you've been encouraged by these same buddies to play in your club's annual invitational. You're a better player than you were a year ago, but you're not exactly sure that you're ready for competition. Heck, most of the guys that you play with are better than you anyway and the odds of you winning a tournament are slim and Slim left town. Shoot, you could end up being paired with the Club Champion -- oh, what a joy that would be. That is why this game has what we call a 'Handicap.'

A handicap is a way of balancing the scales for players of different skill levels. For example, lets say you and your local Club Professional are going to play golf. Assuming that the Pro feels well that day, he is going to be tough to beat. A handicap provides a more equitable condition for this competition. It takes something away from the Pro and gives it to you. Or, more accurately, it takes strokes away from your score to level the playing field.

Let's start out with a common scenario and get more specific as we go. Case in point; suppose that the Club Pro's average score for a round of golf is 70 and we will assume that your average score for a round of golf is 75. This means that to give you the chance to compete with the Pro, you will need to have your score reduced by 5 strokes for each round. This is known as the 'gross' and the 'net.' Your gross score (insert your own comment here) was 75. The Handicap System allowed you to take 5 strokes off of your total score. This translates to a net score of 70. With the Pro's gross 70 and your net 70, you have earned a tie.

This is a very simple explanation. How we arrive at the handicap is more complex. Here is a basic step-by-step introduction into the system. First, to be official, you must join a golf group or club. A player could reconcile their own scores and come up with a number, but this would only be for their own benefit. If a golfer wants to participate in a match, even with a group of friends, the handicap needs to be verified.

In our part of the country, the largest organization is the Northern California Golf Association (NCGA), which works with the United States Golf Association (USGA).

To become a subscriber, or member, of the NCGA, individuals join a local or convenient group. This could be the golf club at your favorite golf course, known as a 'Regular Club'. A group of players, or golf club, that is not affiliated with a certain course is known as an 'Associate Club' (a club without real estate). The NCGA does many things for its Membership and establishing a USGA Handicap Index is one of the benefits.

Once a subscriber, or member, you 'post' your scores after each round. When the round is completed, we enter the data from the round into a computer, which is typically located at the golf course that you just played. Some courses or clubs still use paper and post the scores by hand, but today, most golf courses have computers for posting scores.

Each member has a number, like a Driver's License number, that is used for identification. You begin by entering the number and then follow the computer prompts until you have completed the process.

These scores will be gathered and reconciled to establish a Handicap Index. The NCGA revises Handicap Indexes on a monthly basis (other parts of the country revise on different schedules). Many players wait anxiously for the new release. One score will not result in a verifiable Handicap Index, but you will see some results once you have posted 5 rounds and a revision passes. The System keeps accumulating scores until it has 20. It will then use the low 10 of your last 20 score differentials.

Each round will have a 'differential' between the Rating of the course that you played and your score. Let me elaborate, since this is a bit complicated. Spyglass Hill is one of the most challenging golf courses in the world. Without Ratings a member of this club would have a skewed average compared to the rest of us who play on relatively less challenging courses. So, golf courses are 'rated' to take into account the differences.

These Ratings have quite a few variables. A numerical value is given to obstacles or challenges. I won't go into all of them, but things like length of the holes and size of the putting greens would be included. This adds up to a Course Rating and Slope Rating. Your score, the Slope Rating and the Course Rating are used to calculate a 'differential.' The 'Par' for the course does not factor into the USGA Handicap System.

Here's how it looks on the chalkboard;

Differential =   Adjusted Gross Score
– Course Rating
X
113 / Slope Rating

The aggregate total of these differentials is divided by the number of rounds to come up with an average. A formula is then implemented to arrive at a Handicap Index. This Handicap Index will be 'translated' to a specific Course Handicap for each golf course that you play.

For example, a Handicap Index might be 14.2, that number is then converted to a Course Handicap at each golf course. At the Mediocre Golf Club this same Index would convert to a Course Handicap of 14. However, at Spyglass Hill, this might convert to a Course Handicap of 19. Because the golfer needs more strokes 'taken away' from their total to be competitive.

In practical terms, this is how it plays out. For Stroke Play *(see Chapter 11)* this is a simple net total. The Course Handicap of 19 is subtracted from the total. A gross score of 100 becomes a net score of 81.

The other form of play in Golf is called Match Play *(see Chapter 11)*. Match Play is decided on a hole by hole basis. In this instance, the Course Handicap is divided up between the respective holes on the course. On the scorecard you will notice that each hole has been assigned a handicap number. This is not the order of holes on the course, this is a number used by the Handicap System to distribute the number of strokes allotted to you for that match. These numbers appear to bounce all over the place, first 3, then 15, then 5. They are set-up to give help in order of need. So, at the Number 1 handicap hole the less skilled player will need a stroke (deducted to arrive at the net score) the most to obtain a halve (tie) with the more skilled player.

This is over simplifying, but you'll get the idea. Player A has a Course Handicap of 5, or what we would call 'a 5 handicap.' Player B is a '6 handicap'. Per USGA recommended handicap allowances, the players don't typically use their 'full' Course Handicap in a match. The lower Course Handicap is subtracted from the higher Course Handicap(s) and the balance is distributed.

During their Match, Player B would 'receive' one stroke. This stroke would come into play on the Number 1 handicap hole. The greater the difference in handicaps of the players, the more strokes come into play for that round.

The terminology that will be used on the golf course is a bit of an oxymoron. Because even though we actually take a stroke away from the less skilled player, we call it 'giving them strokes.'

On the golf course you will hear the question, "How many strokes do you get?" Or you might hear an identifying remark like, "She's a low handicap, so she doesn't get many strokes.

HOLE	1	2	3	4	5	6	7	8	9	OUT
BACK TEES 73.9/134	446	535	353	196	363	407	426	587	175	3488
MIDDLE TEES 71.7/129	408	515	323	160	347	316	395	544	162	3230
FORWARD TEES 69.3/120	381	464	294	133	319	351	368	507	141	2958
HANDICAP	5	7	13	17	11	9	3	1	15	
PLAYER A ⑤	5	6	4	3	4	5	4	5	3	39
PLAYER B ⑥	5	5	5	4	4	5	3	6•	4	41
PLAYER B GROSS	5	6	4	3	4	5	4	6	3	39
PLAYER B NET	5	6	4	3	4	5	4	⑤	3	38
MATCH PLAY PLAYER A	AS	−1	AS	+1	+1	+1	AS	AS	+1	

• SIGNIFIES THE HOLE ON WHICH A PLAYER GETS A STROKE

If Player A has a score of 5 on this Number 1 handicap hole and Player B makes a 6 on this hole, they tie this hole. Back to the idea of Gross and Net scores, Player B makes a Gross 6 for a Net of 5 and thus the tie.

Here is a blank scorecard. On each Golf Course, you will have options of how long the Course will play depending upon which set of tees are used. The overall length and the length of each hole are on the card. The 'Par' for each hole is noted. On this card next to the Par are the designations for the Men's handicap holes. Notice that the Forward Tees have their own set of Handicap holes.

CHAMPIONSHIP 72.4/136	MIDDLE 71.3/132	STROKE HOLES	PAR						HOLE			PAR	STROKE HOLES	FORWARD 74.1/139
421	409	5	4						1			4/5	11	409
548	538	1	5						2			5	1	510
162	155	17	3						3			3	17	142
384	373	7	4						4			4	7	366
493	471	11	5						5			5	5	416
518	509	3	5						6			5	3	475
168	161	15	3						7			3	13	155
363	347	9	4						8			4	9	319
292	282	13	4						9			4	15	247
3349	3245		37						OUT			37/38		3039
480	480	16	5						10			5	2	480
437	428	4	4						11			4/5	10	401
404	397	2	4						12			4	8	310
365	343	14	4						13			4	14	285
388	382	8	4						14			4	6	323
143	127	18	3						15			3	18	119
219	219	6	3						16			3/4	16	208
393	382	10	4						17			4	4	355
346	329	12	4						18			4	12	296
3175	3087		35						IN			35/37		2777
6524	6332		72						TOTAL			72/75		5816
HANDICAP														
NET SCORE														
DATE		SCORER						ATTEST						

Sandbaggers... Like anything else in life, there will be some who will abuse the system. Some do this for personal gain, others do it for their ego.

For the player who records fabricated scores, or does not post all scores, he or she will receive an inflated handicap. The player will then play better or worse when necessary to achieve the desired result, and use the handicap strokes for a lower net score. This player is known as a Sandbagger. (note: the Handicap Committee at your golf club can adjust a Handicap Index for manipulating scores or failing to post a score)

Ironically, some players desire a lower Handicap Index than their game deserves. You see, some players measure themselves and others by their respective Handicap Index. Remember, the Index is the base number that we use in order to arrive at Course Handicap for each golf course. The lower the Index, the assumed better player.

It is usually the first question asked after someone finds out that you play golf. "Oh, Joe plays golf? What's his 'Handicap' (or 'Index')?" Some players will feed their own ego by reducing their Index without supporting evidence. They will only post their low scores.

With the Handicap System utilizing the low 10 of the last 20 scores, and having no real high scores to 'throw out', it will produce an unrealistic, fabricated low Index. Of course, they never win a match, but the unrealistic excuses go with it; "I never play this bad" or "I didn't bring my 'A' game." There are terms for this as well, but the disease is 'reverse sandbagger syndrome.'

Golf is certainly a game that you can play on your own, but you're missing out if you're not involved with a group. You don't have to have a lot of money or a great game. As you will soon discover, not too many players have a great game. If you enjoy the game and would like to participate in a group, you need a handicap. At your earliest opportunity, join a Club that will provide you with a Handicap Index. Then sign up for a few events. As you participate, you will become more comfortable and confident. Who knows, you might even gain a few friends along the way.

Chapter 13

PLACE YOUR BETS

After warming up for a few minutes, your tennis partner leans over the net and says, "Hey, how much do you want to play for? How 'bout $5 for each set and $5 to whoever wins?"

This may not occur very often on the tennis court, in your bowling league, or down at the gym, but it takes place everyday at every golf course across these United States. Of course, not every round of golf will contain a wager, however, your wallet and your brain need to be ready.

Here we go -- the Boss invites you out to his Club. He says that he wants to get to know you better. Perhaps the motive is to 'spend a little one on one time' or introduce you to some new clients.

After a few swings on the driving range, you saunter up to the first tee. There are the customary introductions and then you hear, "Hey, what's your handicap? We usually play for five a side with two down automatics." Visibly perplexed, you think to yourself, "Well, my handicap is that basketball injury to my left knee...a side of what?. ...who's a low down what?"

Betting and golf are intertwined. For the veteran, playing without something at stake is little more than practice. The wager makes it real. This is not gambling (although that is available for those who seek it). This is a stake in yourself or your team. Some of you may consider this semantics, but you are not putting money on a horse or a deck of cards over which you have no control. You have an opportunity to put your body and your mind to the test. Granted, this is more of a testosterone thing, but the point is to find out how well we and our competitors will perform under pressure. Heck, we might even win a few bucks.

Take a moment and review Chapter 11 on Types of Play and Chapter 12 on Handicaps. You will need to recall some of this information as I go over different betting games and wagers that you need to know. Remember, in order to look and sound like you know what you're doing, you don't need to know everything. You just need to know enough to say the 'password' -- a few words that will give the impression that you're in the loop. From there, you can always say, "You know, I remember this, but I'm not sure about that". You'll be fine.

The Nassau - This is a three-pronged bet. There is a bet for the Front Nine, a bet for the Back Nine, and a bet for the overall Eighteen Hole round. The value of the stake is usually the same for each prong, but occasionally the overall, Eighteen Hole bet can be worth more. The denomination is negotiable, and for the average player, the amount can be very tame. In fact, for 'seasoned' citizens this was commonly referred to as a '$2 nassau.' Due to inflation, $5 has become the standard.

All right, let's put this to work. Jane and Joe have agreed to a $10 nassau. The form of play is always Match Play. Jane is 1UP after the Front Nine, which means that she has won the first bet. (Let me interject here that payment is made at the conclusion of play. You never know what will happen on the back nine.) This also means that she is 1UP on the overall eighteen hole bet. Joe plays a little better on the Back Nine and they halve the Side (nine holes). So, Jane remains 1UP and wins the overall Eighteen Hole bet. She has already won the Front and the back nine ended in a tie. Jane collects $20 from Joe for the two bets that she won.

The Press - If you want to sound like a veteran or be able to play with those who are known to accept a wager, you must become familiar with a 'Press.' A Press is never its own game and it's not a different game. It is just more 'prongs' or spokes to the same wheel. It is an addition that 'piggy-backs' an existing bet.

Jane is putting a thorough thrashing on Joe. Along the way Joe feels the winds of providence changing. If only he could start over, have a new beginning. In a way he can. Of course, he is the one who got himself into this mess, and he is the only one who can get himself out. He is down on the original bet, but he can create a new bet, another bet, that will give him a chance. An opportunity not only to cut his losses, but also, he could come out on top, if things go well. This is known as a 'Press'. It is a new bet that runs alongside the current bet. If there were one active bet, a Press would make two. The old one is still going, but now there is a new one. They are side by side, betting on the same thing.

In another scenario, Joe is 3 Holes down after playing just five holes. There are four holes remaining on the Front Side of the Nassau and something needs to change quickly. "Will you accept a Press?", is Joe's question. Jane has the option of denying the Press. Shoot, she's beating you fair and square, but in a friendly game, acceptance is the only answer.

HOLE	1	2	3	4	5	6	7	8	9	OUT	10	11	12	13	14	15	16	17	18	IN	TOTAL
YARDAGE	318	411	259	95	269	314	295	48	123	2502	391	328	143	286	320	304	116	374	293	2575	5077
HANDICAP	5	7	13	17	11	9	3	1	15		8	6	18	16	2	4	14	12	10		
JANE	3	3	3	4	4	5	5	4	3			8	5	4	7	4	4	5			
JOE	4	3	4	4	5	4	3	3	2			8	6	4	7	6	6	7			
MATCH +/-	-1	-1	-2	-2	-3	-2/+1 /41	-1/+2 /42	AS/+1 /43	+1/+4 JOE wins 2 BETS	AS	-1	-1	-1	-2	-3	-4					JOE LOSES 2 BETS

PRESS STARTS HERE→

BOTH BETS ARE NOW OVER

NEW BET FOR BACK NINE WITH JOE +1 ON THE 18 HOLE BET

NOW 4 DOWN ON THE BACK NINE & 3 DOWN ON THE 18 HOLE BET — JOE HAS LOST BOTH BETS.

WITH 2 BETS WON ON THE FRONT AND 2 BETS LOST ON THE BACK JOE & JANE BREAK EVEN.

With two bets now running on the 6th Tee, Joe is still 3 DOWN (DN) on the original bet and All Square (AS) on the Press. Joe hits it close and wins the 6th hole. Now, Joe has gained on the original bet and is just 2DN. On the Press, his victory puts him 1UP. If the remaining holes were tied (halved), Joe would break even -- one loss with the original bet and one win with the Press.

However, old Joe, he just keeps hitting great shots and wins the 7th, 8th, and 9th holes. The original bet went from 2DN, to 1DN, to AS, and finally 1UP. The additional bet, the Press, moved from 1UP, to 2UP, to 3UP, to finish at 4UP. Now, Jane has lost both bets and both bets are over. Hopefully, she will regain her form on the back nine where she still has some hope.

A Press should only be applied to a losing bet, and you should not press a bet that is beyond recovery, or what we call 'closed out'. If Joe was 3DN on the 17th Hole, he could not win. It is not equitable to ask for a new bet when he has already lost the original. To combat this, there is an option for the Press to be 'automatic.' Players can decide prior to the Match that when one is down by a certain number of holes, a Press will be applied without request. This can also control the number of active bets.

Without some parameters, these Press bets can get out of hand to the point of humor. People who are playing poorly will Press the original Nine Hole Bet. Then, they will Press the Overall Eighteen Hole bet. Once they are losing those, they will Press the Press. You can see where this is going. When you bet, keep your wits about you. (*Maybe I should rethink my comment about this not being gambling.*)

Everyone has a bad day. You thought the day could only get better, so you a throw a few presses on your opponent. Like a dark cloud interrupting a sunny afternoon, the round goes from bad to worse. With the final hole approaching you realize that, barring a miracle, there is no escape.

In a friendly game, there has emerged a special Press bet for the player or team who has played poorly all day. This wager is not known in every circle, but it is growing in awareness. Saved for the final hole, this bet is a last ditch effort for the losing side to redeem themselves. Knowing it is not equitable to Press on 'closed out' bets, this Press will allow the losing player or team to Press half of the bets on which they are down. They can't get all of it back, in fact they could lose another 50%, but it's an option if you feel lucky. It has been called by different names, but around here it is known as the 'Aloha Press'.

The handy 'cap -- Handicaps may be applied to each Match. This can be done in two ways. The first is to 'spin' off of the lower handicap. You subtract the lower handicap from the higher handicap and apply the balance. The second way is to use 'Full' handicaps. The entire complement of handicap strokes is applied to each golfer.

My advice is to 'spin' off the low 'cap'. I say this primarily because the Handicap System is set-up for the higher handicap to receive strokes on certain holes in the order of importance. If the strokes are applied at 'Full Handicap', the balance will fall on a different selection of holes.

What if you want to play multiple matches? Maybe you want to have a match with everyone in your group, but your wallet content is in question, and you'll need a CPA to keep track of the side bets and presses. Over the years, different games have evolved with the intention of allowing three or more players to participate in one Match.

SKINS - You know as I write this, I realize that I do not know why we use the name 'Skins.' The prize is one Free Golf Lesson to the person can give me the real answer to that question. Anywho, this is essentially a Match Play format for groups of three or more players. The difference is that once a player has won the hole, it cannot be taken from him/her. It is not tracked by a player being 'up', 'down' or 'all square.' You simply account for the number of holes that are won and by whom. To win a hole is to have won a 'Skin'.

There are two different forms of 'Skins' games, with variations that can apply to either type. Each year, in the fall (specifically Thanksgiving Weekend), there is a made for TV event which is appropriately called the 'Skins Game'. Four world famous players get together and play the game for someone else's money -- big money. We're talking $50,000, $60,000, or $70,000 per hole. If no one wins that hole, the money is then 'carried over' and the next hole is worth the total of the two. If no one wins that hole, the new total is again 'carried over' and joined with the value of the following hole. This continues until a player wins a 'Skin.' Then, the next hole is worth its sole value. This is known as Progressive. In the event of a tie on the 18th hole, there is a 'playoff', or extra hole(s) until the final Skin is won.

This 'progressive' form of Skins can be enjoyed by anyone. It is fun to have the pressure build, as consecutive holes are tied, and the value of the next hole continues to mount.

However, for the other 35,000,000 non-televised golfers, there is not always on opportunity for a playoff. The greens fee applies to 18 holes and that's it. As a result, these unclaimed holes simply are not accounted for.

This brings up an argument against this 'progressive' type of Skins. Why should the value of a hole change? Should a skin that is won after seven successive ties be more valuable than a skin won on the 1st hole? Should a winning score on a one certain hole have more worth than any other winning score? A score of Par could have a greater reward than that of an Eagle. Not too mention the accounting, especially if you have multiple groups playing in the same game.

Sometimes the way to go is simply to play for the Pot. Each player puts a Federal Reserve Note in the Pot, or for you Poker fans, we ante up. When a player wins a Skin, he/she wins a piece of the Pot. There is no need to worry about a tie on the 18th hole. All Skins have equal value and the math is easy. Especially, if only one player wins a Skin, then that player gets it all.

Now, you might be thinking to yourself, "Gee, someone could get lucky and play well on one hole and win the entire pot." First of all, I admire your insight. Secondly, there is a plan. This option is called 'validation' or 'confirmation'. With this as part of the game, a player who wins a Skin must follow it up with a certain level of play on the next hole. This 'validation' could be simply making par. Or, it can be as difficult as not being out-played on the next hole -- not that you have to win two Skins in a row, just a tie will do.

RABBITS, SQUIRRELS, & GOPHERS -- Although similar to a Skins Game this game is a closer kin to Match Play. The principal difference is that when playing a Rabbit, your 'Skin', or what we call a 'leg', can be taken from you. Again, this is a format used by three or more players and can be used by multiple groups. A Pot, or value, is established and you're ready.

Think about it like it is a form of Match Play. At the beginning, everyone is equal or 'All Square.' In terms of the game, we are trying to 'catch' the rabbit and the rabbit 'is running'. When someone wins a hole he/she is 1UP, but you need to use Rabbit (or even Skin) terms, so you have won a 'leg'. The object of the game is to end with a 'leg', or to possess more 'legs' than the amount of holes that remain. Remember, however, that you do not have a single opponent. Everyone that you are playing with is now trying to take that 'leg' back from you, because in the end (you run out of holes) the player with the 'leg' wins.

What happens if a player with the 'leg' wins another hole? That player now has two 'legs.' This is good, because if you lose one 'leg' (by losing the hole) you still have another 'leg.' Don't lose that one though. When no one has won a 'leg' or the 'leg' has been taken from someone, the Rabbit is on the loose and is now 'running.'

The game can last throughout the entire 18 holes or you can create smaller sections. A popular way to segment the game is to play three Rabbits that contain 6 holes each. These smaller Rabbits create a possibility for more than one winner, or if a golfer is playing well, he/she might win all three. There is no need for 'validation', a player validates by retaining the 'leg'.

Oh, what are Squirrels and Gophers? A twist on the Rabbit is to pay out double if the 'leg' is won with a Birdie (squirrel), and triple if won with an Eagle (gopher). There must be some historical relevance for using names of burrowing animals.

If anyone can provide me with the genuine answer, I'll put up another free lesson for the first correct respondent.

Here is an important note as we wrap this section up. Although all of us want to improve our scores and become better players, this Chapter is not exempt from the previously unwritten rule: It doesn't matter how you play, its how you look.

My point is, that as you get your feet wet, don't be too afraid of a few early losses. First off, your handicap may be used to create a level playing field. It isn't like you will be expected to play mano-a-mano with Sergio Garcia. Players of all levels are accustomed to either 'giving' or 'getting' strokes depending on the players in their group. Of course, like anything else in life you can always try to negotiate. This should make you feel a little better.

Secondly, we're not talking about big money, these stakes won't get any higher than twenty bucks. This is probably half of the amount that you paid for your greens fee. Heck, the biggest thing you have to lose is your ego.

Finally, even good players lose. That's just the way it goes. The winner of the match doesn't even complain. I have yet to hear someone say, "You know, I was really offended. Joe lost the match and paid me five dollars." Heck, the only problem you might have is to make sure that your boss doesn't think that you were *trying* to lose.

This is certainly a good foundation for money games on the course and, as always, puts you in a position to talk a good game. There are many games, but these are the most popular. Don't be worried if someone comes up with a word or phrase that you've never heard of, no one is an expert on everything (although we all know someone like this). Become familiar with these games and terms, and you will be in the loop.

Chapter 14

GOLF INSTRUCTION

An old, wise Golf Pro had a sign on the counter in the Golf Shop. It read,

SERIES OF SIX LESSONS

$150

ONE GOLF LESSON

$1000

After walking into the shop, players would read the sign and ask, "If six lessons are $150, how can one lesson be $1000."

With a wry grin he replied, "If you want a miracle, you're gonna have to pay for it."

The time is NOW. This answer makes me feel a little like the 'Carnack the Magnificent' skit that was done by Johnny Carson. The question that you were about to ask is 'when should I start taking Golf Lessons?'.

Let's take this from the back-end. Who is the last person that you would think needs a golf lesson? That question could be expanded. Who are the last 125 people in the world who would need a golf lessons? The everyday, usual score for these players is under par. A large number of these players drive the ball over 280 yards off the Tee. Normally, their ball will come to rest on the green, in less than two shots, 14 of the 18 holes. Over the course of their round they will average less than 2 putts per hole. More often than not, a ball that lands in a Sand Bunker will be in the hole after two shots. If you're thinking the exempt players on the Tour, you would be right. Maybe you should be Carnack the Magnificent.

In many cases, these players are visited by their Instructor everyday. These days, if an Instructor has to miss an appointment (instructors have more than one player) in this hi-tech world, the Player can send a digital image of his/her swing. The Instructor will then critique the swing, possibly compare it to another swing, and respond with advice.

Are you with me? If the best players in the world are receiving Golf Lessons and those who know nothing about the game need a guide, then everyone needs to receive PGA or LPGA Instruction.

If you are currently hooked up with an Instructor, good job. If not, here's some information regarding different types of Instruction and how to choose a PGA or LPGA Professional.

Private Lessons: This is one-on-one Instruction with the Professional. This is the most effective learning environment. You have the undivided attention of your Pro and you are able to focus without the distraction of others. Once you have chosen a qualified Instructor, the only challenge to this process is the cost. Depending on the Professional, 30 to 60 minute lessons will have a price of between $40 to $100 at your local Golf Course. For those interested in pursuing the Tour, the cost goes up quite a bit. We're looking at a top-rated Professional that you've never heard of for a few hundred dollars an hour up to a world renowned Instructor that won't accept a new student for less than $5000.

Chances are in a matter of months, many of you will spend over $300 for a new driver, or maybe $1000 on a new set of irons. A greens fee at the local course will be at least $20 and probably more like $50, each time you play golf. Puts that $40 in perspective doesn't it. You'll get that back in found golf balls.

Semi-Private Lessons: These are very similar to the Private Lessons, with more than one student involved. The value of the lesson is proportionate to the number of students involved in the lesson. As the number of students increases, the amount of time that the Instructor is able to spend with each one decreases. However, this type of Lesson is ideal for family or friends to learn together. Also, it will spread out the cost between 2 - 4 people. The rates will be in the same range with the Private Lessons, but the cost will break down to less per person.

Group Lessons: If your budget doesn't have a lot of room for golf or you just love to be with a Group of people this is the way to go. The obvious drawback is that the Instructor is not able to spend more than a few minutes with each individual. Typically, each session is an hour long and the topics are fixed. For Juniors or those who know very little about the game, a Group Lesson will give them some pertinent general information and the opportunity to put it into action.

Golf Schools: These are usually expensive, concentrated Instruction Programs. They are often held at Resort-type locations, complete with accommodations, golf course and practice facility. The Staff should be top-notch and the Instruction that you receive is often very good. Attendees are assembled into groups and the schedule is predetermined. One drawback is that you can't take the Instructor back to your hometown for a follow-up lesson. Also, it is difficult to quantify how much of the information you are able to retain. But, hey, if you love golf, don't have the time except on vacation, and feel that you are able to absorb the info and have the funds in the family budget, I'm sure it will be a fun week.

The Right Instructor

When enrolling in a Group Lesson or Golf School, one is generally not in a position to choose Instructors. You fill-out the form, pay the fee and attend your first class. Private and Semi-Private lessons give you the opportunity to pick your Instructor. How do we pick the right one?

You need to do some research and there are a couple of ways to begin your quest. First, the old-fashioned way, head on down to the Golf Course of your choice and ask for information about their Golf Instruction Staff. Option B, for those cruising on the Information Super Highway, would be to surf the Web. We can find out quite a bit about local and national Instructors on the Internet. Not only will the Golf Course have a few bytes dedicated to their Teaching Program, but also some have developed Golf Instruction 'Brokers' (for the lack of a better word) that have a listing of PGA/LPGA Professionals that are in your area.

What are the qualifications of the Instructor? Like dating, there is no way to guarantee a match with your potential Instructor, but you can narrow the search. Make sure that he or she is a Member of either the Professional Golfer's Association (PGA) or Ladies Professional Golfer's Association (LPGA). Although it is not the sole objective of the respective organizations, the PGA and LPGA have the highest standards for those who attain Membership. There are other organizations who will put out a crop of 'graduates' who are able to teach. They have snazzy names like America's Best Teaching Academy, but the high standards aren't there.

How long has the Instructor been Teaching? If this is a Group Lesson, the experience won't be a big factor, but in a Private Lesson you want to get what you pay for. You should look for a minimum of 3 years.

What is the Teaching Philosophy of the Instructor? Depending on where you are in your golf timeline, this may not have a lot of influence on your decision. Ironically, the answer should also be more about you and not all about them. At the same time, if the response is something like, 'well, the swing doesn't matter, its the power of positive thinking', then you can eliminate that Instructor. The idea here is to get the Instructor talking. Can the person communicate thoughts effectively?

Ask if it would it be possible to get a reference or speak with one of his/her current students? This might be a little over the top, but you never know.

Put all of these ingredients together and go for it. PGA/LPGA Professionals that work at your local Course, have taught the game for a few years, are able to explain to you what path the lessons will take, odds are good that this will work for you.

Have you noticed that I have not even mentioned the Instructor's playing ability? Not that the ability to play precludes one from being a good Teacher, it's just not necessary. The Instructor that you have chosen is a Member of the PGA or LPGA, so they have to be able to play a little bit. How often **they** play is not going to help **your** play.

Video

You may have wondered about the advantages of Video Instruction. The way that you think your swing looks and the way it really looks are different. You may think you like Jack Nicklaus, but chances are you swing like Jack Nicholson. Sometimes, when people see their swing, they become so concerned with how they look, that it messes with them. Video has its place. The naked eye can't see everything and an Instructor might need to be able to slow things down a bit. Also, at times a student will not understand or truly believe something the Instructor says until he/she sees it. Just take it slow. Video lessons should be few and far between. Most of your Instruction should be without pictures, unless you need some convincing or the Instructor needs to take a closer look. It is more important that you can feel the correct motion than to get too caught up in what it looks like. When it comes down to and playing well and game improvement, there are no pictures on the Scorecard.

Finally, everyone needs a little help from their friends, but the best way that your friends can help your golf game is to watch. Relegate them to the role of moral support. Too many cooks in the kitchen, too many bowls spoils the broth, take your pick for the analogy. The issue is that you don't want to receive a lot of trivial information. You want to locate a narrow source for solid information. Find a good Professional, give some purpose to your practice. Then let your friends ask if you've been taking lessons.

Chapter 15

PRACTICE

When I was young, I would hit sand shots for hours. The local course, where I worked, had a bunker and practice putting green situated just outside the golf shop. During one of my marathon practice sessions a very good senior player walked by (it was not unusual for him to 'shoot his age' -- he was 75 and his score was 75). He told me, "You just keep doing what you're doing. In time anyone can hit a golf ball straight. What people cannot do is get the ball in the hole." That was one of the best pieces of advice I have ever heard.

You already know that you need to practice. What you don't know is how to practice and when you will find the time. At this juncture, I will only be able to help you with the 'how to' part. I am not going to go into a lot of specific content about the swing, that will be between you and your instructor, my objective is to provide a system. It will be a format or template that you can use to practice like a pro and stay focused during your session. How often you practice and how quickly you improve is very individual, but first you do need to know how it's done.

When you dissect your golf score or any golf score for that matter, you will find that at least half of the round is made up of shots that are hit within 50 yards of the hole. Really, during your next round, take a moment after each hole and jot down some notes on the scorecard. Record how many full swings. Next record how many chips or pitches. Finally, make a note of how many putts. When you're finished playing, tally them up. What did you get? I'll bet it was more *short game* shots than *full swings*.

Now, next time you're at the golf course, take a look at the Practice Areas. That driving range will have an array of people making full swings and the short game area or practice putting green will have a handful or people (at the most), and that handful is only there because they are about to go play and just want to get a 'feel' for the Greens. The area of the game that deserves at least half of our practice time (if not more) is often given the back seat. Don't get me wrong, I understand that chipping a ball near the hole is not as sexy as the booming drive, but when you post your score, it is a cold fact.

My objective in this chapter is to provide a good overview of how to practice and the encouragement to be consistent about the time that you dedicate to it. It should give you some fodder, something to chew on. Then it is up to you. One thing that you can invest is time and golf will give you a good return.

Within the context of this book, my goal is not to create tour players. I am not suggesting that you call in sick everyday and go to the nearest practice facility. However, to fit in with (and become) the veteran player, you must grasp the *importance* of practice, *how* to practice and *what* to practice. Actually, let's pause here for a moment and make a distinction. There are some who play the game for a long time and don't intend to improve.

The term 'veteran player' does not apply to them. We might call this the 'casual golfer'. With all due respect, fitting in with the casual golfer is not the concern. You want to be able to converse with and be respected by the veteran, be respected by your clients, and be a better player in the future. You need to set aside some time to hit balls and understand an effective plan to use that time.

Truly, there is no single way to practice. Players will develop, by design or default, their own routines or agendas. Your personality will be seen in the way that you practice. An engineer might be very structured in a practice session, while an artist may be more concerned with balance and rhythm. This will be up to you; I just want to help you with some of the groundwork.

When you are trying to improve you game, practice will be fun and challenging. Naturally, on occasion, it will be more challenging than fun.

Together with your Instructor, you will come up with drills or exercises that will help your swing become more mechanically sound. Sometimes, when you're being challenged, these motions and positions can feel very awkward for weeks. It is important that you blend or intertwine this mechanical side of your practice with some more comfortable, rhythmical motions that will give you a break.

When you're swinging well, most of your time will be spent in the efforts of 'routine maintenance'. This will be composed of a review of some basic motions that you are trying to repeat and the ongoing mission of rhythm, comfort, and good balance.

Here is a template for a solid practice session:

FULL SWING

- Always start off by warming up. Everyone's body is different. Take your time and let your muscles move around a little. You might consider a certain amount of stretching. A bench or one of your Golf Clubs can be used to limber up your arms and legs.

- Take a moment and set a couple of golf clubs down on the ground that will align you toward the target. Tour Players do this everyday, so you will look like a veteran. This gives you one less thing for your brain to think about.

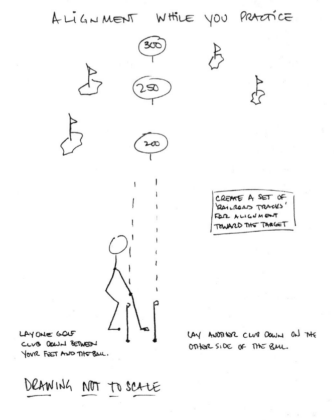

ALIGNMENT WHILE YOU PRACTICE

300

250

200

CREATE A SET OF 'RAILROAD TRACKS' FOR ALIGNMENT TOWARD THE TARGET

LAY ONE GOLF CLUB DOWN BETWEEN YOUR FEET AND THE BALL.

LAY ANOTHER CLUB DOWN ON THE OTHER SIDE OF THE BALL.

DRAWING NOT TO SCALE

- Make a few swings without the ball. It's a good idea to begin with one of the shorter clubs. Choose a wedge or maybe an 8-iron. Start with small swings and work your way up to full swings.

- Next, use the same approach with the golf ball. Let smaller motions graduate into larger motions until you are finally making full swings. Go ahead and hit 8 - 10 balls with full swings. At this point, you should be ready to begin.

- Bear in mind that the average range bucket will hold about 60 - 70 balls and you will probably need 40 - 50 balls to work on something specific.

- Your Instructor has undoubtedly given you some valuable information that you need to put into action. Use your drill or exercise. Don't misunderstand this isn't militant. Try some, and then take a break.

Speaking of breaks, lets pause here. We all come to the game with prejudice. Not necessarily in a bad way. It's just that we all have a preconceived notion (mentally) of the swing and what it should feel like (physically). This time is allotted for the introduction of new concepts or motions into your golf swing. Each day, as your trust in the new information builds, the uncomfortable will become more comfortable.

Let me give you an example. In my golf swing, my hands tend to manipulate the golf club just as I am taking the club away in the backswing. This is not good. It would put the club in a bad position. Using an exercise, or drill, from a renowned Instructor, I began to feel the right thing. The only problem was that the old way was so ingrained, the correct position felt awful. My brain and body did not trust this new position.

In this portion of my practice, I would use the drill twice. Next, I would make five full-swings, then take a brief break. Use the drill twice, then make five full-swings. The goal is to bring the new position in at regular intervals. If you go 'cold turkey,' you won't see much success and will get frustrated. Go back and forth. Give the new motion or feeling or position some time to acclimate. Like transferring fish from one bowl to another, you give the water some time to let the temperature level out.

During this 'homework' part of your practice you should stick with a cozy golf club -- ideally, a #6, #7, or #8-iron. The fact of the matter is that the longer the golf club the more difficult it is to hit a solid shot. Usually, the 'homework' isn't designed to use a long iron or wood. You want to experience some success with these new motions before we test them on the longer clubs.

For the last segment of my practice, I would stop using the drill. In fact, I will remind myself that the drill is done and take away the golf clubs that were used for alignment.

- Leave the mechanics of the exercise and focus on the rhythm of the swing. Use those last 10 - 15 balls to rehearse good balance. And in my swing specifically, I want to ensure a steady, solid finish.

- In the final portion, go ahead and use a variety of clubs. Hit a few woods, the return to the irons. Finish up with some steady, balanced iron shots and your session is complete.

I mentioned before that there would be periods of time when you're swinging pretty well and you won't have the 'homework' portion. This can be replaced by some target practice. Use markers on the Driving Range to create a fairway. Challenge yourself to hit the fairway. If successful, choose an iron and try to hit one of the greens on the Range. If available, use your wedges, and see if you can hit the flagstick (even the Pros don't do that very often).

SHORT GAME:

Whether you prefer to make full swings first or would rather hit a few putts to start off, half of your practice should take place near or on the putting green. Even if you are not working on a specific technical issue, you need to chip quite a few balls and sink several putts every time that you practice.

Of course, the correct, fundamental motions that you are learning on the driving range will carry over and help your short game shots as well. However, this area of the game will require more art than machine from your golf swing.

- Drop a few balls around the hole at point-blank range.

- Make sure that you are aligned correctly, and then roll them in.

- After 8 - 10 putts, move further away from the hole.

- Once you have hit these putts, move to about 20' away.

- From this distance, some of the balls might finish more than 2' away from the hole. On the golf course, there is no guarantee that these short putts will go in, so we want to practice them here first. In fact, you might go through an 'on course' type routine before you putt these. Place a coin behind the ball, lift the ball, replace the ball, and then hit the putt.

Next, find an area to chip a few balls:

- Begin with a Sand Wedge or Pitching Wedge and a very comfortable distance.
- Hit 8 - 10 balls. Gather them up and repeat.
- Pick a new hole with a different distance, and then hit 8 - 10 chips.
- Change clubs. Using anything from a #6 iron to a Lob Wedge, vary your distances and choose different hole locations. Hit 8 - 10 each.
- Here is the test: Choose one club, one hole, and one ball. Go ahead and hit the chip. Now, take your putter and see if you can make the putt.

Like the full swing on the driving range, you do not want to fool yourself into thinking that everything is always going fine. You want to vary your distances and change clubs and choose new holes. Then when you feel confident, put it to the test. See how many times that you can hit just one chip and one putt. This is known as getting 'up and down'.

Without homework, you need to keep your mind in your practice. The last thing that you want to do is hit balls without purpose. In the Chapter on Lessons I remind you that the goal of Golf Lessons is to give purpose to your practice.

The next challenge is to take your improvement on the driving range and implement it onto the golf course. This isn't always a smooth transition. It can be like getting into a swimming pool. You put that foot in, and then you take it out. Back in it goes, this time it stays in. You know the drill: knees, waist, until finally all of you is in the water. Once you're in you think, "Hey, this isn't so bad." Trusting your swing on the golf course can also feel a bit chilly, until you feel more comfortable.

Ultimately, on the golf course, before striking the golf ball, you want to say to yourself, "I'm prepared to hit this shot, I've hit this shot a hundred times successfully on the Driving Range and I'll be successful here, too!"

Chapter 16

WHAT DO YOU NEED?

How many times have you made a purchase only to discover that it was the wrong thing? We go to the hardware store for a tool to fix the Widget 2000. Upon returning home, we find that this tool will only fix the Widget 3000. We all have a shelf or drawer (or room) that becomes the graveyard for these items.

Over the next few pages I will show you how to head these poor purchases off at the pass. Granted, golf equipment is a billion dollar industry with hundreds of vendors and thousands of products and new marketing comes out every year. Still true, however, is the Biblical information that 'nothing is new under the sun.'

Vendors know that the average golfer is looking for the quick fix or the magic lamp. Just rub this new driver, the genie will come out and grant you three wishes. Some of these claims can be real or they can be a mirage. The fact of the matter is that competition for golf club sales has increased dramatically over the last thirty years. As a result, many vendors have become convoluted and confusing in their effort to be unique. In this chapter, I will discuss some keys in the effort to avoid the purchase of Aladdin's lamp.

"Gee, I think that I will buy the cheapest thing that I can find. Who knows, maybe, I won't like this game. Heck, it doesn't matter what I play with anyway, I don't know what I'm doing yet. If I do end up liking this game, that's when I will spend some money on something good." Sound familiar?

We have relatives who are frugal to the point of being foolish. After countless hours of research and procrastination, the fatal purchase is made. It seldom fails, the item will break, wear out, not fit, or be the wrong widget. It truly is a remarkable thing. The end result is to spend twice as much and still have a second-class product. Now, you don't have to go buy a Lexus, but at the same time you want to avoid the Yugo. You can spend a reasonable amount, receive a quality product, and get it right the first time.

Frankly, my objective is two-fold; give you enough information to do the most with your money and, yes, ensure that you will present a veteran image.

Lets go through this categorically, in order of importance.

CUSTOM FITTING: When you buy shoes, you choose the correct size. When you buy skis, you choose length, type, and flex, based on your weight and ability. The golf clubs that you purchase should fit you as well. There are many ingredients to the recipe and although its possible to be more detailed, I will limit this overview to four basic issues: shaft flex, club length, grip size, and lie angle.

The Flex of the Club -- Believe it or not, when you swing a golf club, the shaft will flex. The amount of flex in the shaft is very important, because it directly affects the relationship between your hands and the clubhead. This relationship is paramount. Of course, this is not something that you should think about when you swing, but nonetheless, it is happening, and its position is crucial to your success. A buggy whip would be too flexible. A piece of lumber would be too rigid.

Each player needs to have the correct amount of flex for their own swing. People with more strength and better technique should use a less flexible shaft. They create their own flex and in turn, clubhead speed. Clubhead speed means distance. They don't need distance -- they need to be able to find the ball. A 'stiffer' shaft will help them keep things under control.

Golfers with less strength and less clubhead speed need a shaft that is more flexible. For the lack of a better phrase, the shaft will flex for them. This 'loose' shaft will help them to generate more club-head speed hit the ball higher and drive the ball a greater distance.

The Lie of the Club -- Another valid concern is the position of the club head. Idcally, the angle between the shaft and clubhead will allow the golf clubhead to be level with the ground at impact. When a player prepares to hit a shot, it is possible to see whether or not the bottom of the clubhead is level. This is a practical example that is easy to see, but more important, is the clubhead position during the swing. Most players will be at one position before the swing and in a different position, or angle, during the swing. With each golfer, we need to make a measurement, and potentially an adjustment with the club, so that the angle of the clubhead is correct.

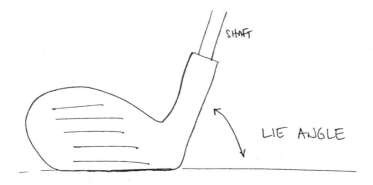

This is called 'lie angle.' As is true of other categories in club-fitting, the industry came up with a 'standard' for this angle. To sound like a veteran, we talk about changes to 'lie angle' with 'standard' as a base. Adjustments to the standard measured in degrees. An alteration that is higher than standard is known as 'upright', with lower than standard being called 'flat'. For example, if the shaft angle needs to be two degrees higher, it is known as being '2 up'. The other side of that coin would be called '2 down'.

The Length of the Club -- Simply put, the overall length of the club should be measured and needs to be correct.

Remember your parents, telling you that something was too much of a good thing? This is what you need to know about length. The longer the golf club, the more clubhead speed can be generated. This can mean greater distance for your golf ball. However, the longer that clubhead gets from you, the less control you have. You will hit the ball a long way (assuming you can achieve solid contact) and never find it.

This means that most players do not want their clubs to be more than a 1/2" or so away from standard. Women pay attention. Often, a less than experienced club-fitter will want to make women's golf clubs much shorter. The explanation will be ball control or the toe of the club is pointing up in the address position (lie angle is too upright). Forget control, let's keep the length and adjust the lie angle. Over the last fifteen years of teaching and playing I have never heard a female amateur looking for control -- what everybody wants is distance. Once you have played the game for a year or so, you will be able to find your golf ball virtually every time you hit it. Ironically, that is part of the problem, you don't hit it far enough to get into trouble. You want that golf club long. As long as you can handle it. Simply have the lie angle adjusted, and you're good to go.

The Grip of the Club -- This is often overlooked, and yet for me, its one of the big four issues. A player's hands need to be able to move as they should in a golf swing. Golf club grips that are too large for one's hands tend to restrict motion and grips that are too small tend to move around during the swing. Have you ever grabbed a screw-driver only to find that the handle is so small you can't rotate the tool real well? Once you have a larger handle it feels a lot better. Be careful though, if it's too big, you can't get a good grip on it. Grips are available in different textures and sizes. It will be no problem for a reputable manufacturer to dial you in to the perfect grip.

In summary, when you purchase a set of irons, you want to accomplish two things. First, go with a reputable brand and your local Club Professional, who will stand behind the product. Second, the golf clubs must fit you. Don't use Uncle Ralph's Widget 2000 that he bought 10 years ago. Don't let a junior golfer use Dad's old golf clubs (or worse cut them down). Please, head down to your local Golf Shop and let your local Club Professional fit you for a new set of clubs. If the family budget will not allow for that, still go through the fitting process and get your specifications. Then search for a used set that will match these specifications a closely as possible.

GOLF CLUBS -- If chosen wisely, a golf club could last the rest of your life.

Irons: Essentially, there are two types of irons. One type, the *traditional clubhead* is very simple in appearance. It is a solid piece of metal with descriptions like; blade, muscle back, fat back, or square back.

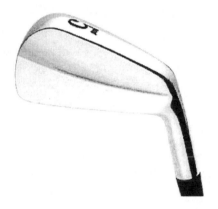

The main benefit with the 'blade' is that the ball has a more acute reaction with the clubface. Historically, the material begins as a larger piece of carbon steel and 'forged' into a clubhead. This material is relatively soft and the ball will 'stay on the face' of the club longer. We are talking about fractions of a second, but when the golf clubhead is traveling near one hundred miles an hour at impact, every little bit helps. As a result, the ball will spin at a higher rate.

A myth spread in certain circles demonstrates a golf ball moving up the face of the club and using the 'grooves' (or score-lines) to produce spin. During the swing a golf ball simply does not have the time to do this. Often rebounding off the clubhead in less that 1/10th of a second, the ball is well on its way before it had a chance to move up or down the face of the club.

Grass that is between the clubface and your golf ball at impact will cause problems. In ideal conditions, the grooves aren't even necessary. The ball makes unimpeded contact with the face and the result should be true. It is in the less than perfect situation that we need them. The grooves give the grass a place to go. Of course there will still be some grass between the ball and the face, but you have a reasonable shot at hitting it solid.

With the traditional 'blade' type of clubhead, this additional spin allows better players to have more control over the movement of the ball. To sound like a veteran, this is known as 'working' the ball. If a skilled player would like to make a swing with the intent of moving the ball to the left or to the right it is called 'shaping a shot'. This is more easily done when using this type of club.

For example, a ball that is struck correctly with the intention of a 'draw', will move from the right side of the target then back left toward the target (for a right handed player). A 'hook' is a shot that will travel from the right to the left, but with more severity. The opposite would be a 'slice', and the more controlled shot that moves from the left to the right, is known as a 'fade.'

Another benefit from the 'blade' is what the advanced player will feel when the ball strikes the clubhead. Golf clubs are designed for the golf ball to hit the clubhead in the middle of the face. When a ball is struck correctly, in the middle of the face, there is a message sent from the clubhead. It travels through the shaft of the club, up to your hands, and from there to your brain. At which point your brain understands -- that felt good. Its almost like you didn't hit anything at all. This is called the 'sweet spot'. For those of you who play other sports, you may know what I'm talking about. Tennis racquets have a sweet spot. Baseball bats will send a similar message.

The dilemma is that with this traditional type of club, that spot is only about the size of a dime. Everything else is what we call a miss-hit. When this occurs, the golf club will twist (to varying degrees). This twist and off-center contact cause a vibration that you will feel in your hands. Naturally, this has other adverse effects. The most important of which are a loss of distance and accuracy. Unfortunately, the more you miss, the greater the loss. When a ball is hit offline, but struck in the middle of the clubface it will typically hold that line. With the off-center hit, if the ball is hit offline, it now moves even further offline and is usually coupled with a loss of distance. Each off-center shot has a similar cause and effect.

You might begin to recognize that the traditional 'blade' clubhead that is enjoyed by the advanced player for feel and control, is unlikely to be enjoyed or controlled by the average player. In the past, this was the only type of club available. Today it should be reserved for the skilled player. Few of us are at this level and some people have made the advanced player purchase without first possessing the skills necessary to use them. Miss-hit shots will occur on a regular basis. Heck, the ball might be missed completely on occasion. Be not dismayed. There is help.

In the 1960's a brilliant guy by the name of Karsten Solheim started to experiment with clubs in which the weight of the head was reworked or redistributed to the perimeter of the clubhead. This is known as 'cavity-back' or 'perimeter weighted.' A cavity was created in the rear of the clubhead and allowed the weight to make a rim around the outside.

Therefore, if the golf ball does not hit the center or 'sweetspot' of the clubhead, there is more support. Here is a dramatic example using a tennis ball. Imagine playing tennis with a ping-pong paddle. What happens if the tennis ball hits the edge of the paddle? That paddle will wobble all over the place. It might even get knocked right out of your hand. Now, imagine that you're using a modern tennis racquet. The weight around the outside of the racquet will help off-center hits. The racquet will still vibrate, but you will be able to hit the ball and you won't lose as much distance or accuracy.

One of the early prototypes of this engineering was a putter. The putter had the weight removed from the middle and redistributed to each end. The thing looked like a shaft with a small rectangular box at the end of it. It wasn't pretty -- it was practical. When the ball hit the face of the putter it made this high pitched pinging tone. This sound became synonymous with the model and the brand became 'Ping'.

Woods: There are fewer decisions to make when it comes to woods. The lie angle is not as critical here. In fact, most manufacturers don't have 'lie angle' as an option. Although distance is the factor in the forefront of our minds, you don't need to be as concerned with length of the club. You see, with the irons, consistent distances are the concern. As you improve, you will find that we don't want our 7-iron to travel five yards shorter or farther from one swing to the next. This could mean the water in front of the green or the bunker in the back. With the Driver, you don't need to be too concerned with a five yard variable, you just want it to hit a solid shot.

Categorically, there are Drivers and Fairway woods. Not to say that they are mutually exclusive, they are named for their common use. In one of life's cruel ironies, the clubs that will hit the ball a greater distance are the most difficult to control. Truth be told, I often recommend that players use the fairway woods off of the tee until they become more comfortable with the driver.

Drivers are defined by degrees. In the old days, you would simply have a Driver, or #1 wood, followed by a #3 wood and a #5 wood. You will see this same configuration in many outdated sets at your local course. Now, nearly all woods are identified by amount of angle on the face. This is called 'loft'.

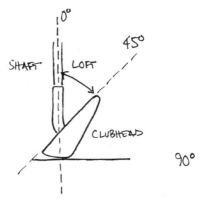

LOFT ANGLE ILLUSTRATION - DEGREES

Loft is established by counting the number of ticks from top dead center, which is '0' degrees. The horizon, or perpendicular line, would be at 90 degrees. So, an average 10° driver is ten ticks from center. Drivers are available in a variety of degrees, but men should stick with something close to 10° and women should use 12° for the first couple of years.

Fairway woods are designed to hit the ball off of the turf. The bottom, or sole, of the club is more rounded and the weight within the head is set up to encourage the ball to fly higher. Thankfully, most vendors still include the traditional number next to the degrees of loft printed on the clubs. When you're set is complete, you will have a #3 wood, #5 wood and a 'trouble' or high lofted club like a #7 wood. Certainly, if your budget or your commitment doesn't allow, the first choice should be #3, and then #5. This will give you a more versatile, multi-purpose club that may be used off of the tee or fairway as you see fit.

Most clubs are made of steel, due to cost. Principally, the two materials used are steel and titanium. Titanium is lighter and harder (clubhead speed and distance) and naturally more expensive. If you can afford a Titanium Driver, go for it. With the fairway woods, the difference is not as significant, so don't waste your money. At this point, something worthy of note is that they are still called 'woods' even though they're not made of wood anymore. Some have tried a conversion to calling the steel or titanium clubs what they are, which is Metalheads or Fairway Metals. Unfortunately there are too many syllables. Sounds lazy and it is, but if the name, Alex Rodriquez, turns into A-Rod, I'll just stick with '3-wood' instead of '3-fairway metal.'

Shaft material will be our final golf club topic. A hundred years ago, golf club shafts were made with hickory. Steel shafts brought a lot of consistency to the game in the last century. Over the last twenty years, graphite has been gaining prominence. The main sell being its light weight. The draw-backs of graphite are cost and consistency. Light-weight Steel shafts are not much heavier than graphite and they are more consistent and less expensive. Graphite's advertised difference is greater distance, but from my experience the real issue is how the shaft feels. This difference is realized in the off-center shot. With a graphite shaft you will feel less of the gonging vibration that is felt with the steel shaft when you miss the center of the clubface.

For your driver purchase, wallet allowing, go for the graphite shaft and the titanium head. It is a little lighter and larger, so you may gain some distance and it will feel better. To keep the cost down and get the consistency for the 'scoring' clubs, go with steel in the fairway woods and your next set of irons.

SHOES: You get what you pay for. Although there are a gazillion available styles and models from the dozens of different vendors, I will distill this down to three basic types. Here we go:

All Leather: This is the classic golf shoe. Like a comfortable dress shoe, this type has a primarily leather sole and a leather upper. The support of your foot is solid, the natural material breathes, and it provides the look of the Tour Pro. Several years ago, these shoes were not available in waterproof, so we had to save them for the dry days. Now these shoes are available with two-year water-proof guarantees and are a good pick for every season. MSRP $150 - $300

Leather Upper / Synthetic Sole: Most players today wear this type of shoe. It has a traditional leather upper, but with a synthetic sole. When it comes to producing a waterproof shoe, this made things easier for the vendors. In fact, there are some styles that come with three-year waterproof warranties.

Because the sole is synthetic, shoe-makers have experimented quite a bit with materials. Graphite, gel, and encapsulated air, have all been used for either comfort or stability. This can be a very solid choice in a very broad category. Remember, to avoid looking for the Genie in the lamp here. Stick with a top brand (Foot-joy, Nike, Adidas, Dexter, Etonic) and spend slightly more than you think you should spend. MSRP $75 - $225

All Synthetic: This is the category for the golfer who only plays a handful of times a year and is frugal to near foolishness. The only way that I could recommend this shoe is if the person plays only on February 29th and lives in the desert. Okay, maybe that's extreme, but you get the point. Be careful, if you buy a shoe without waterproof guaranty and make sure that you spend less than forty bucks, because for another $15 you could upgrade into the next category with one of last year's close-outs. MSRP $40 - $60

GLOVES: With materials similar to shoes, there are two basic categories;

All leather: This all natural material will allow the glove to 'breathe.' With hot weather and the moisture from our hands, this is important. Also, the leather is soft and has a better feel with the golf club.

The down-side is that this type of glove will be more expensive and yet not have long life. As with many other products (tires, racquet string), the better the material the shorter the life expectancy. Real good leather gloves are very thin and have a real soft feel. MSRP range $15 - $30

Synthetic: These gloves will last longer than the leather, for sure. They will also be less expensive. Frankly, if you can't tell the difference, this is the way to go. Some vendors will even go so far as to put a leather patch or two on a couple of primary contact points. However, you are still touching the synthetic, and it makes the glove feel thicker.

Probably, the best reason to go with synthetic can be the fit. Many vendors today have spent some time in research and development and come up with ways to help your glove, well, fit like a glove. With spandex or lycra type webbing and incisions in just the right places, a growing number of these synthetic gloves feel just right. MSRP range $8 - $15

BALLS: In the twentieth century, this would have been a much longer monologue. Balls were made in two ways. One was like a baseball, with an inner liquid-filled core. This was wrapped by windings, and then a cover. The other was a simple, larger, solid inner core without windings, followed by a cover. We called them 'wound' and 'two-piece' respectively.

WOUND   **TWO-PIECE**

Today, the 'wound' ball is almost a relic. Golfers no longer need to inquire, "Gee, what compression should I get?". Golf balls aren't damaged due to a simple miss hit. Variations of the 'two-piece' ball have taken over the Tour and the Industry. Their playing characteristics are more consistent.

The material difference is the material. One of the golf equipment conundrums is the attempt to satisfy two needs within one ball. Golfers yearn for more distance off the tee. However, when around the greens players are not looking for distance. The desire is for a ball that is softer and more responsive. Vendors have come up with exotic substances and can produce a ball that travels further, yet they can perform like a softer ball for short game shots around the greens. Granted, the more hi-tech the material, the more hi-tech the price.

Balls are sold primarily in dozens, or can be broken down into three-ball or four-ball containers that are called 'sleeves'. For the top-shelf balls its near $50 per dozen.

This doesn't mean that you can't find a quality ball at an affordable price. There are many 'upper middle-class' golf balls out there for around $35. Usually, this class of golf ball is slanted toward the distance side of the scale. The feel around the greens won't be as good as the top-shelf ball, but it is still a quality product.

Or, for those of you who don't care or at this point can't tell the difference, there are many bargain balls available in dozens and 15-ball packs for $20. At this level you are going to receive a monolithic 'distance' ball and the quality control may not provide for consistent distances or reactions, but hey, until you notice the difference, keep playing them.

For the veteran maneuver in the ball category, either play an 'upper middle-class' ball or higher. If the budget doesn't approve of this find some Titleist's in the 'experienced' ball section of the local golf shop. Sometimes called 'water balls' due to their place of origin, these seldom used golf balls with an unknown pedigree are available in buckets or boxes in many pro shops around the country.

Of course they are not 'certified pre-owned' and there is no transferable warranty, but they are worth the price at pennies on the dollar.

That is a lot of valuable information. Now, you are not only in a much better position when it the time comes for you to make a purchase, you are also prepared to engage in a conversation with the golfers in your group.

Being a billion dollar industry and knowing the psychology of the yearning golfer, you will discover many different products from a variety of vendors. The most important thing that you can do is keep it simple. There is nothing wrong with buying the club, ball, glove, or shoe that has a proven track record. In fashion terms, the polo shirt and a pair of khakis will never be out of style. Let someone else be the guinea pig for all of the new stuff.

Locate a well-known, reliable product and go for it. For a list of my current recommendations, just get online and go to www.intheloopbook.com.

Chapter 17

AN INTRODUCTION TO RULES

Offsides, Icing, Illegal Crackback, these are a few rules from sport that require some investment in the game to figure out what they are and why they exist. Golf has a few of these, too.

There is one important thing to remember. The objective is for all who will play, to play by the same rules. Regardless of your age or ability, the parameters do not vary.

Although there may be moments when we do not understand how a certain rule may come to be, when can rest on the fact that many, many hours have been invested over the last two hundred years to arrive at the decisions and documents that we have to day.

The Gentleman Golfers of Leith wrote the original thirteen rules in the year 1744. Here they are:

1   *You must Tee your Ball within a Club's length of the Hole*

2   *Your Tee must be upon the Ground.*

3   *You are not to change the Ball which you Strike off the Tee.*

4   *You are not to remove Stones, Bones, or any Break Club for the sake of playing your Ball, except upon the fair Green, & that only within a club length of your Ball.*

5   *If your Ball come among Watter, or any Wattery Filth, you are at liberty to take out your Ball, & bringing it behind the hazard, and teeing it, you may play it with any club and allow your Adversary a stroke for so getting out your Ball.*

6   *If your Balls be found anywhere touching one another, you are to lift the first Ball till you play the last.*

7   *At Holling, you are to play your Ball honestly for the Hole, and not play upon your Adversary's Ball, not lying in your way to the hole.*

8   *If you shou'd lose your Ball by its being taken up, or in any other way, you are to go back to the spot where you struck last & drop another Ball, and allow your Adversary a stroke for your misfortune.*

9   *No man, at Holling is Ball, is to be allowed to mark to the Hole with his Club, or anything else.*

10 *If a Ball be stop'd by any person, Horse, Dog, or anything else, the Ball so stop'd must be play'd where it lyes.*

11 *If you draw your Club in order to strike, & proceed as far in the stroke as to be bringing down your Club, if then, your Club shall break in any way, it is it be Accounted as stroke.*

12 *He whose Ball lyes farthest from the Hole is obliged to play first.*

13 *Neither Trench, Ditch, or Dyke made for the preservation of the Links, or the Scholar's holes, or the Soldier's lines, shall be accounted a Hazard; but the Ball is to be taken out / Teed / and played with any Iron Club.*

Pretty straightforward, eh? If your dog or your horse stops your ball, that's the way it goes. A phrase developed over the years, its called 'rub of the green'. We still use that one. By definition, Rub of the Green occurs when a ball in motion is deflected of stopped by any outside agency. This would include dogs and horses. You hit it. You find it. You play it.

Today, the Rules of Golf have grown to a total of 34. And over the years, we have come up with enough 'but what about this' and 'if I could just...' comments to require more detail in writing the rules. In fact, we now have a companion book known as the Decisions on the Rules of Golf' book. This is a compilation of interpretations and clarifications for unique situations.

Naturally, regulations can occasionally cramp your style, but there is also a certain amount of redemption for those who know the rules. You may find your ball in an adverse position from which you are entitled to relief. That's right, no penalty, just move the ball to a different spot, in accordance with the Rules. A few of these rules will come up in nearly every round of golf that you play.

There are some veterans who take pride in their knowledge of the Rules of Golf. We will not try to impress them. Ironically, it's more than likely, that you would get into their good graces by asking a few questions. One of the reasons that he/she wants to know the rules is so that everybody else will know that they know the rules.

Ironically, there are some very good players, tour players in fact, that do not have a good grasp of the rules. So, you won't look silly if you are not sure what to do in every situation. At the same time, you don't want to get into a discussion on the Rules of Golf or play a round of golf totally ignorant.

We will not go into all 34 Rules of Golf. Nevertheless, to give some depth to your knowledge, you will need to have a general idea where to look for an issue in the Rules of Golf book and you will need to be familiar with the Definitions section of the book. These two things go together, when you are comfortable with the Definitions set forth in the book, they will answer many questions that you have and make it easier to find answers in the book.

Rule 27 - Ball Lost or Out of Bounds; Provisional Ball - Simply put, what do you do if you can't locate your ball, or your ball has been hit off the course? It's not in water. You just cannot find it or you saw it fly into that some guy's backyard. There is only one thing to do.

R.27-1 - If a ball is lost or out of bounds, the player must play a ball, under penalty of one stroke, as nearly as possible at the spot from which the original ball was last played'. That's it. Only option. It is rude, to tacky, to at worst cheating, to walk up to where your ball may have been, or might have flown over the fence, then drop another ball and play it.

"But," you say to yourself, "what if I am looking for my ball and then realize that it is out of bounds or cannot be found?" Let me address a couple of things here. First off, nearly all fences, walls, buildings, homes, etc are considered 'out of bounds' (O.B.). According to the Definitions (remember those Definitions) OB is not even part of the golf course. So, if your ball is in the air moving over a fence or toward a row of houses, it is a safe assumption that the ball will come to rest OB.

If certain that this has happened, here is the procedure. Tell the players in your group what is going on. Take another ball, hold the ball at arms length and at shoulder height and drop the ball as near as possible to the original spot, but no nearer to the hole. If the ball that was hit OB is your tee shot, you may place it on the tee again. So, we hit the ball out of bounds. That's one stroke. Under the Rules, we are penalized one stroke. Your next shot is stroke number three. This penalty is known as 'stroke and distance.'

"But," you say to yourself, "what if I am not sure the ball is OB, I don't want to walk all the way down there, not be able to find it and have to walk back to hit my next shot." Which, brings us to our second point. The Rules of Golf do provide for a 'what if'. This is called a Provisional Ball (Rule 27-2) The ball that we just hit is flying toward the fence. We don't know if it is on the golf course or is out of bounds. Without penalty one may play another ball provisionally' until the doubt surrounding the original ball has been erased.

Again, notify you're the other players as to what you are doing. It will sound like this, "That one might be out of bounds. I am going to play a provisional ball." If you find the first one, that's great. Put the provisional ball in your bag. The original ball remains the ball in play. If you don't find the original, the provisional ball becomes the ball in play. You do receive the penalty, but you don't have to walk back to the tee.

Water Hazards - Rule 26 - Any sea, lake, pond, river, ditch, surface drainage ditch, or other open water course (whether or not containing water) and anything of a similar nature' on the course. Well, that narrows it down, doesn't it. Yellow or red stakes in the ground define these areas. A ball that is in this condition may be played and unless you're wearing your Sunday best, I say, "Go for it!" But usually it's not possible to play it and we need to know what to do.

Similar to the out of bounds scenario, you do receive a penalty. There is good news, however, you don't have go back to our original location to hit your next shot. Move all the way up to the margin (border) of the hazard and hit from there. By the way, you've got options; A) you can play the ball from the original spot, or B) if the hazard is a lateral water hazard (runs more along side of you, than in front of you), you can drop to either side of where the ball crossed the margin (line) of the hazard, within two club lengths, or C) keeping the point where the ball went into the hazard between ourselves and the hole, you can walk as far back as you want and hit from there. Determine your best option and drop your ball. Assuming the original was your first shot, it is counted as 1. The penalty is counted as 2, the next stroke will be number 3.

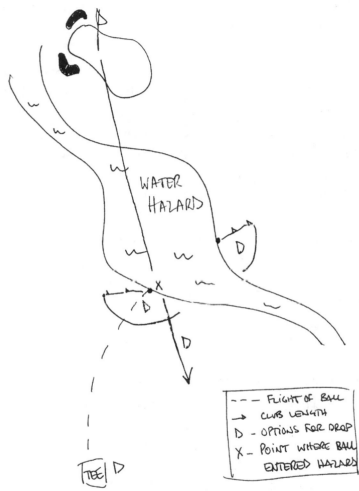

WATER HAZARD

	FLIGHT OF BALL
→	CLUB LENGTH
D	OPTIONS FOR DROP
X	POINT WHERE BALL ENTERED HAZARD

TEE D

WHERE TO DROP IF YOUR BALL ENTERS A HAZARD

One more Rule of Golf to go over. This one is going to help you a lot! Throughout your round you might encounter a variety of situations that will make the game even more difficult if you don't know how to address them.

"A tour player would be jealous", is your thought as you gaze longingly down the fairway. Your ball plummets to earth, appears to bounce, but disappears from view.

It was nearly three hundred paces, but it seemed weightless until the reality hit you. "Where's my ball?" The search and rescue unit was about to give up hope when a small, white shell is visible in some soft ground. Our career drive is now nearly submerged and certainly unplayable. What can be done?

Knowing the following rule can help. Whereas most of the golf course allows the ball to bounce and come to rest above the level of the ground, the above scenario is covered by **Rule 25 - 'Abnormal Ground Conditions, Embedded Ball Rule and Wrong Putting Green'.** Generally speaking a ball that is involved in a debilitating accident is given a reprieve. Termed 'relief' in the Rules, there are situations in which a player is able to 'lift' the ball without penalty, move to a reasonable location and put the ball into play.

The scenario described above is an embedded ball. A ball embedded in its own pitch-mark in the ground in any closely-mown area through the green, may be lifted, cleaned and dropped, without penalty, as near as possible to the spot where it lay but not nearer the hole. Casual Water' is covered by this Rule as well. This is a temporary accumulation of water' that is outside of a water hazard. Maybe the rain just stopped and the course has some areas that have not fully drained or evaporated. If water is visible before or after your stance, you are entitled to relief.

This is a simple, brief explanation of just 3 of the 34 Rules. Although these will come up on a daily basis, there is much more to know. Frankly, like the physical aspects of the game, the education is ongoing.

Your knowledge of the Rules of Golf may help you out of some negative situations, but more than that you will be able to play the game as it should be played. There is honor and integrity woven into the fabric of those who have a vested interest in this game.

At your earliest opportunity, purchase a copy of the Rules of Golf. Your local golf shop should have them in stock. If not, a visit to www.usga.org or a search on the internet will put one in your hands within a day or two.

Remember, I want you to have enough knowledge on the Rules of Golf so that you will be able to be fair to yourself and to others when you play and know enough about the origins of the Rules that you will be 'up to speed' or even impress the players in your group.

Chapter 18

WALK THE WALK &
TALK THE TALK

What is a byte? For that matter, you can have a lot of bytes, kilobytes, or megabytes. They must have been really hungry. A person can get really confused looking for a computer. One word, memory, is used with more than one definition. There are gigahertz, hard drives, software, 2.4 this and 5.3 that. Most of the time we just nod.

We have all been told that there is no 'dumb' question, but in certain circles, you don't want to be relegated to the role of student. You want to be ahead of the game. You want to fit in.

Golf, like other industries, has its own vernacular. You've probably heard the individual words before, but this time the words have an entirely different meaning. There are phrases that are understood only in the context of experience. Saying the words may not even be enough; you might have to say them the right way.

There are many sources for finding the definitions to often used Golf words. The most readily available would be your home computer. On your favorite Search Engine, type in 'golf glossary.'

My purpose is to go beyond that, or maybe around that. Don't get me wrong, you will need to know many of those words, it's just that we want you to sound like an insider. Anyone can use the words already in the Dictionary. I want you to know the phrases and verbiage that you probably won't find anywhere else.

For the most part, this book is a glossary in and of itself, but over the next few pages I am going to explain some unique verbiage. I will even throw in a few words and phrases that are not so well known. These will get you 'over the hump' if you feel uncomfortable. By using the seldom known word or phrase, their perception will be that you know the secret hand shake, or you've bought the decoder ring. Just because you missed some of the other code words doesn't matter, you are still on the inside.

Here are some phrases that are common in the veteran world; they might sound a bit unusual if you aren't familiar with them:

'Golfed' or 'Golfing' -- Let me start you off with a very subtle, but dead give away to the inside the industry or veteran player that they are speaking to the novice or intermediate player. Never used the word 'golfed.' In fact, we do not use the word 'golf' as an action word. Bowlers bowl', but golfers do not 'golf.' They 'play golf.' Bowlers go bowling,' but golfers do not go 'golfing.' They go play golf'. You may now be perplexed. It's okay, that is why you are reading this book. In the English language the words make sense. They might even be grammatically correct, but don't say it that way. To my knowledge, this is not written down anywhere (until now). Just be glad I told you.

If you are going to ask someone to play golf, you say, "Hey, do you want to play golf on Saturday?" Always insert the word 'play.' You are not 'going golfing,' you are going to 'play golf.' Or, you can really up the ante by using the word 'round.' "Hey, do you want to get a round of golf in on Saturday." In fact, when talking to a veteran the only word you need is round,' he/she will know. In the same manner, to the veteran, the past tense of golf is not golfed'. The veteran would say, *played* golf.'

"Did you guys play golf the other day?"

"...Yeah, we played a few holes."

"Did you play 18 (holes) or 9 (holes)?"

"It was getting dark so we only played 9."

"How'd you play?"

"Oh, I played alright..."

These are all correct phrases (and a downright typical conversation).

'You're away' -- The rules and etiquette of the game state that the next player to hit is the one who is furthest from the hole. This is simply informing a player that it is his/her turn. On this note, the question 'who's away?' is the best way to ask who is next to hit.

'Golf Shot' -- Of course you can say 'good shot', but it doesn't have quite the veteran undertones. You have condensed a sentence into this tidy little phrase.

'Its a good angle from there' -- Unless you are in a group of old friends, stay away from virtually any remark that follows a partner's bad shot. However, in the event of uncomfortable silence, this is a good one to keep things light if a shot should go astray.

Quacker -- When a right-handed player hits a ball off the tee that goes low and left, it is a severe hook that we call a 'duck hook'. Again, part of being a veteran is using a non-conventional word for a conventional situation. So, as the phrase 'duck hook' became conventional, it is now being replaced with a similar but not-so-conventional, 'quacker.'

Stiff or Stony -- This is in reference to a shot that has come to rest very close to the hole or flagstick. Granted, these two words are more in use by the younger crowd, but you need to know what it means. Ironically, the word 'close' still remains the choice for most of us when someone hits a shot near the pin.

Drano -- A ball can go in the hole from any distance, but this word is reserved for the long putt. You don't say 'Drano' for a putt that should go into the hole over 50% of the time. It comes from the idea of something going down the drain or hole.

Flier -- Now we know that most of the balls that are hit result in the ball flying. However, this word defines a ball that is struck with a normal golf swing, but travels a greater than normal distance. On the fairway, this will not happen. In the rough, however, long, dry grass can gather between the golf ball and the club-face. The ball will not spin as it should and cause a knuckle-ball like effect. The result will be the ball traveling farther than you intended. Along with this word, there is also the phrase 'catch a flier' or passed tense 'caught a flier.' It would sound like this, "That ball just landed somewhere in the next county, I must have caught a flier."

Hacker -- For the computer industry, this word is used for someone who is intelligent, but is doing something that he/she should not be doing. In golf, however, this is the word that describes a poor player. Like anything else in life, if someone admits their deficiency we are more than prepared to accept them, but if they are unaware or unwilling to admit this, they are just a 'hack.'

Jail -- We all know this as a place that we do not want to go. From there we can see freedom, but we are caged. Your golf ball might enter situations like this. Most of the time, you don't want to get greedy. You just want out. You might hear, "Where's Fred?" "Oh, he sprayed one right. He's in jail."

Spray -- After that last sentence, I had better follow-up with this one. When you put your finger on the aerosol can and push, where does it go? Lets just say it's not very precise. So, when you 'spray' a shot on the course, it's usually not easy to find.

Bagger -- This is actually a shorter version of the popular word 'sandbagger.' Crossing lines between sports, this refers to someone who consistently posts scores (see Chapter 12: Handicaps) that are higher than his or her skill level. This causes the player's handicap to remain high and he/she can easily play at or below it.

Shank -- It was very hard for me to type that word. Quite possibly a virus, it can be spread by casual contact. So contagious is it, that we do not even say the word. This is the 'reverse' glossary word, a word that you should never say. Whether fact or fiction, I don't care. This word describes a result of cataclysmic proportions. The ball hits near the hosel or neck of the clubhead and the ball flies laterally rather than forward. It feels awful; you have no idea how it happened, where it came from, or where it will go. We have come up with replacement words, however, the most popular of which is the 'lateral.'

Heavy or thin -- When the clubhead makes unintentional contact with the ground prior to hitting the ball, we call this 'heavy.' When the clubhead hits high on the ball, but the ball still flies, we call this 'thin.' These well-known words have spawned words for the insider. We say 'fat' and 'chunky' or 'anorexic' to say the same thing without saying the same thing.

Loop -- A round of golf is also known as a 'loop.' This has been an insider word for a long time, but never seemed to become conventional. It might be because we seldom use it to describe the round of golf. It is used to describe those who make the trip on an almost daily basis, but never hit a shot. A 'looper' is the veteran term for caddy. Also known as 'packing,' one who carries two bags (private club thing) becomes a 'double-packer.'

A topic worth commenting on at this point is the conversation, albeit one-sided, that you should have with your golf ball. It may seem ludicrous to speak to an object, but I can assure you that there will be times when it seems that the ball can hear. Of course, there will be other instances in which that ball will lose all ability to heed your beck and call. However, you don't want to let an opportunity pass you by. When your ball is headed 'elsewhere' go ahead and shout.

'Bite!' -- When your target is the green or more specifically the flagstick and your ball is certainly going to go too far (or 'long'), this is a good command. You see, when a ball is spinning at a high rate, and hits a green, it often will not bounce very far. In fact, adept players will be able to have a reasonable amount of control over this action. Balls will hit and stop, or the spin may even cause the ball to come back toward the player. This is the background on the word 'bite.'

A quick note here. Generally speaking, veterans do not use the word 'stop'. Part of being a veteran is the use of clever verbiage. You can even make up your own, but be very careful a missed attempt could be fatal. The word 'stop' is simply too normal.

'Get down!' -- This is a more general term that can be applied to any airborne golf ball. You really don't want this ball to fly anymore.

'Flaps!' -- What does a plane do when it is preparing for landing? Reduces air speed, Gear Down (hey, you might hear that one, too), flaps...We want that ball to land and stop.

'Fly!' -- Also, a command for the airborne ball, this directs the ignorant object to stay in the air.

WHO'S WHO

Some of the most intriguing and stimulating conversations that you will have at the Golf Course will be about golf's legends and golf's greatest shots. Many of these great and legendary moments have been global: Gene Sarazen making an Eagle 3 (two under par for one hole) at Augusta National's fifteenth hole on his way to win the Master's Tournament, a 71st Hole chip-in by Tom Watson to beat Jack Nicklaus in the U.S. Open, several years later it was Jack shooting 30 over the last nine holes at Augusta to win the Masters (at the age of 46).

Just as many memorable and legendary moments will be very local. These will include your own great shots, your own moments, and your own legends. This is one of the reasons that we play the game. Each day, each round, every shot, has the potential to gain legendary or celebrity status.

Let me take this opportunity to nip something right in the bud. Please do not tell details to others about your specific round of golf. Tell them your score or a quick generic response. It might go like this, "Hey, how'd you play today?" *"Oh, some good, some bad"*, or *"Pretty good, I almost broke 100,"* or *"Well, I was hitting my irons alright, but I couldn't make a putt."* Keep it short.

The last thing you want to do is answer this question with a hole-by-hole, shot-by-shot recitation. We all love each other and we all want to see each other do well, but nobody wants your four-hour round to be re-lived right in front of them. If you tell a story, it better be good. Of course these memories and stories might only be entertaining to you and those you play golf with. This won't bother you; because you don't want to hear their boring golf stories either.

I don't tell you this to dampen your fire. I want you to look and act like a veteran. Veterans don't go around telling stories about themselves. Everyone else tells stories about them. This is an irony of golf and life. No one wants to hear someone tell a story about himself or herself, but everyone will listen to a person tell the story about someone else.

In fact, this is how you know it's legendary, when someone else tells your story. It doesn't even matter if its good or bad press. The fact that they're telling the story lets you know that you're in the loop. If you drive a golf cart into the lake (assuming it wasn't staged), hit a ball that ricochets off a house and into the hole, or make a birdie in a hailstorm, any of these will do.

Initially, few of these stories will be about you. So when you talk, talk about another player's game. Ask a few questions. Recall their good shots. Do a lot of listening. You will get into the flow in no time.

IT'S A WRAP

Around the world, there have been many great stories, and each generation has its golf legends. What I have done for you in this book and more specifically in this chapter, is to describe a few names and places and provide you with a good supply of words that will help you in the conversation.

In the space that is available, I cannot go into all of the possibilities, but this section has put some arrows in you quiver. This will enable you to use some words or phrases that will identify you as more than the casual golfer and will also allow you to understand more of what the other veterans are saying.

Our English Dictionary changes every year. Not only do new words enter, but also existing words have alternate definitions. Who would have thought that 'bad' or 'sick' could be regionally accepted as very positive words? The world and language of golf has a similar evolution. Even the veterans don't know them all. Only the Golf Shop Staff does.

THE 19TH HOLE

I am excited for you. Some of you have been playing the game for quite a few years. Others of you have just recently touched a club for the first time. However you arrived at this point, I am pleased that you are here.

I hope that this book has put you more at ease about playing the game regardless of your age or ability. Of course we all want to be better players, but we don't have to be a great golfer to have fun on the course.

Now you have enough information to carry yourself like a veteran on the course. Being a veteran in the game gives you a certain amount of confidence and also allows you to be humble. There is no need for pretense. No one has ever played a perfect game.

You can take pride in the fact that you possess a great deal of knowledge and are part of a magnificent culture. Also, you should realize that the game was here before your involvement and it will be here when your grandchildren are your age.

Golf has often been called a microcosm of life. You can find out a lot about a person over the course of eighteen holes. How do we handle adversity? How do we interact with others?

In one of golf's unique attributes, no competitor can truly overcome another. Whether you play alone or in a large tournament, it is the golf course that we play.

Travel around the globe and you will not find two golf courses that are the same. This is not a bowling alley or a racquetball court. Every golf course, every day, is a new experience. In Palm Springs, green golf courses will be framed with the sands of the desert. The Sierra Mountains will provide stunning back-drops and challenging elevation changes for many golf course designs. A large water hazard will come into play as several golf courses are situated along the California Coastline.

This is the greatest game on earth. You are a part of it. It has been my pleasure to present this digest of stories and information that will make the game more enjoyable for you. I trust that you will play the game often and if you pay attention, you will learn something in each round of golf.

So, go for it. Invite your friends, impress your clients, get that raise, negotiate the deal, but most of all, have fun on the course, because you are ready to get in the loop!